True Crime Storytime

12 Disturbing True Crime Stories to Keep You Up All Night

True Crime Storytime Volume 1

M. Moore, True Crime Seven

TRUE CRIME 7

Copyright © 2020 by Sea Vision Publishing, LLC

All Rights Reserved.

All Rights Reserved.

No part of this publication may be reproduced, distributed, or transmitted in any form or by any means, including photocopying, recording, electronic or mechanical methods, without the prior written permission of the publisher, except in the case of brief quotations embodied in critical reviews and certain other non-commercial uses permitted by copyright law.

Much research, from a variety of sources, has gone into the compilation of this material. We strive to keep the information up-to-date to the best knowledge of the author and publisher; the materials contained herein is factually correct. Neither the publisher nor author will be held responsible for any inaccuracies. This publication is produced solely for informational purposes, and it is not intended to hurt or defame anyone involved.

ISBN: 9798549342033

Table of Contents

Introduction *13*

I Ruth Snyder and Henry Judd Gray *17*

    A Housewife From Queens 18

    Lonely and Looking for Love 20

    Murder for Momsie? 22

    Ruthless Ruth 23

    A Bad Breakup 25

    The Dumbbell Murder Case 26

II Henry Moity *29*

    A Startling Discovery 30

    The Moity's 32

    Husband on the run 34

    Confession and Contempt 36

    Husband on Trial 37

III Nannie Doss *40*

The Giggling Grandma 41

Trading Marriage for Murder 42

Gruesome Grandma 44

Racking up the Body Count 45

The Black Widow Confesses 49

IV Paul Pappas *52*

Jealousy Gone too far 53

Christmas day Disappearance 54

The Lady in the Ashes 55

V The Broadway Butterfly Murders *58*

From Rags to Royalty 59

Sugar Daddy of Death 61

Blackmail or Robbery 63

Another Butterfly Falls 65

VI Buried Alive: The Story of Marie Billings *67*

LA in the Roaring Twenties 68

Bludgeoned and Buried 69

VII Leopold and Loeb 74

Fortunate Sons 75

From Minor Robberies to Murder 76

Pre-meditated Murder of the Highest Degree 77

Confession of a Senseless Crime 82

VIII Hinterkaifeck Murders 86

Footsteps, Bad Feelings, and Fear 87

A Disturbing Discovery 89

Secrets of the Skulls 94

IX Turtle Lake Murders 95

From Well-To-Do, to Dead 96

Baiting a Killer 98

Confessing to the Crime 101

X William Edward Hickman 105

Dangerous Deception 105

Ransom and Religion 108

Capture and Confessions 111

XI Louise Peete *116*

    A Southern Belle 116

    To Murder, not to Marry 118

XII Man in the Attic *124*

    A Bored Housewife and a Secret Boarder 124

    Attic Man Commits Murder 128

    The Captive Comes Clean 130

Conclusion *133*

References *135*

Acknowledgements *137*

I A Troubled Boy *141*

About True Crime Seven *149*

Explore the Stories of
The Murderous Minds

A Note

From True Crime Seven

Hi there!

Thank you so much for picking up our book! Before you continue your exploration into the dark world of killers, we wanted to take a quick moment to explain the purpose of our books.

Our goal is to simply explore and tell the stories of various killers in the world: from unknown murderers to infamous serial killers. Our books are designed to be short and inclusive; we want to tell a good scary true story that anyone can enjoy regardless of their reading level.

That is why you won't see too many fancy words or complicated sentence structures in our books. Also, to prevent typical cut and dry style of true crime books, we try to keep the narrative easy to follow while incorporating fiction style storytelling. As to information, we often find ourselves with too little or too much. So, in terms of research material and content, we always try to include what further helps the story of the killer.

Lastly, we want to acknowledge that, much like history, true crime is a subject that can often be interpreted differently. Depending on the topic and your upbringing, you might agree or disagree with how we present a story. We understand disagreements are inevitable. That is why we added this note so hopefully it can help you better understand our position and goal.

Now without further ado, let the exploration to the dark begin!

Introduction

IN THIS BOOK WE DELVE INTO THE WARPED minds of some of history's most gruesome killers. The 1920's were no stranger to bloodshed, but the gangster murders committed by Al Capone and the like can be considered tame to the events you are about to read.

The 1920s encapsulated a decade of booming wealth, political change, and liberation from former generations values. Affluent families led glamourous lifestyles characterized by stylish vehicles, fancy clothes, and nights spent out on the town. Young women exercised their freedoms both socially and, in the workplace, finally unshackled from strict expectations in regards to their place and propriety.

The nation possessed a zeal for life and a passion for all it had to offer. At night, vibrant culture spilled out of speakeasies and up and down the streets. When the sun rose in the morning, word of the nights previous escapades, including cold-blooded murderers, captivated the public and controlled media attention. Our dark tales of the twenties includes such psychopaths as:

Leopold and Loeb: Geniuses turned child killers who believed themselves above the law. They sadistically planned out their killing for months and expressed little remorse for their actions.

Nannie Doss: A seemingly loving grandmother who murdered over half her family. She ruthlessly exterminated her husband, her mother, her children, and grandchildren.

The Turtle Lake Murders: An entire family brutally slaughtered save for an eight-month-old baby. The murder is believed to have stemmed from a feud between neighbors, but to this day the identity of the true killer is questionable.

The Attic Man: A lonely housewife who convinced her lover to live in her attic for years, unbeknownst to her family.

Chilling, gruesome, and often deeply disturbing, the murders of the 1920s stain the Jazz Age era like blood on sheets. We've combed newspapers and media coverage to give you, our reader, as much information about each killer, details of the crime, and if possible, insights into their dangerously deadly thoughts.

Are your prepared to peek into the psyche of ruthless murderers?

I
Ruth Snyder and Henry Judd Gray

A TALE OF TWO LOVERS SO CAPTIVATING IT WAS turned into a film. Ruth Snyder is played by the alluring Barbara Stanwyck and the charming Fred MacMurray as Henry Judd Gray. Though the 1944 crime noir movie attracted audiences and won the acclaim of critics, the real-life scenario was nothing to be praised.

Nevertheless, the true affair and murder did consume the public's thoughts and hold their interest for quite some time. A love so passionate the couple was willing to commit murder. It was scintillating.

Ruth and her lover would eventually meet the same fate, on the exact same day, death by electrocution. Their stories and lives are forever entangled. They would continue to capture the public's attention even beyond death.

A stolen photo of Snyder's last moments, taken by a camera hidden in the pant leg of a newspaperman, was run on the front page of the Daily News. The issue sold out in just fifteen minutes. The pair, which the movie *Double Indemnity* was based on, wanted anything but notoriety; however, they achieved it in spades.

Here is their sordid tale.

A Housewife From Queens

New York City in the Jazz Age. The setting of the Great Gatsby, home to gangsters and speakeasies, a playground for the rich and famous. Well, at least in the wealthier parts of the city.

The population of Queens nearly doubled in the 1920s. The subway system expanded, the automobile grew increasingly popular, and newly-built bridges made the borough much more accessible.

For some families, like the Snyder's, an address in the Queens neighborhood was a move up in life. You were on your way, one step closer to the parties, the wealth, the celebrities. Unfortunately, Ruth Snyder didn't share her husband's sentiments and this was the beginning of the end. Mr. Snyder's final scene would close with him being bludgeoned, suffocated with chloroform-soaked cotton, and strangled with picture frame wire.

Ruth Snyder was born Ruth Brown in 1895. Where she would eventually find herself living with her husband and daughter wasn't too far from her place of birth, 125th Street, Manhattan. Her Scandinavian parents were average and of the working class. Like many immigrants of the time, they got by and that was enough.

But Ruth had higher aspirations. She completed the eighth grade and then left school; forsaking a formal education for a job with a telephone company. At night she took classes in both shorthand and typing. While she was a hard worker and one would believe she was determined to make a living for herself as a single woman, Ruth said she always "thought more of marriage than [of] a business career."

Little did she know, her ticket to success was closer than she could have imagined. At nineteen, Motor Boating Magazine offered her a secretarial position. Ruth was dedicated but she was also spunky and lively, described as "gay" and "fun-loving." A product of the 1920s, she possessed the energetic freedom and sometimes risky behaviors of her feminist peers, the flappers of the Jazz Age.

It is no surprise then that the magazine's art editor, Albert Snyder, was intrigued by the company's new sassy secretary. At thirty-two, he was thirteen years Ruth's senior, but she didn't mind his attention in the least.

She had far less experience than Albert in the romance department, a fact that may have contributed to the events to come. Albert was Ruth's first true "gentleman friend," and after courting for a few months they were engaged and shortly thereafter married.

At twenty years old, Ruth was now a housewife. It would be three more years before she was a model Queens housewife, the envy of her fellow secretaries.

Ruth's aspirations of being a businesswoman slowly faded away. She was preoccupied with taking care of the home, then she became a mother. The couple named their daughter Lorraine and needing a bigger space, upgraded to a larger Bronx apartment.

Albert was successful at the magazine and was soon able to surprise his wife and child with an impressive eight-room home in Queens Village on Long Island. The Snyder family had finally arrived. Only, for Ruth, the ticket was to a lonely suburban life of cleaning, cooking, mending, and caring for her daughter.

Lonely and Looking for Love

Friends and acquaintances would eventually tell the papers that by 1925, Ruth possessed "everything that most women wish for." Meaning, a house, an automobile, a radio, good furniture, money in the bank, protection, and an athlete for a husband. Albert was a good man and a faithful husband. He took pride in his wife, his child, and his home. He made little things to decorate the house and he was thrifty, but he also worked hard and late.

Sadly, friends and family failed to see that this model husband was also evil-tempered and pessimistic. Ruth's mother got a glimpse behind the rosy curtain when she moved in with Ruth and Albert. Her daughter loved to go out, was cheerful, and sociable while her son-in-law was gloomy, a homebody, and generally uninterested in anything Ruth was.

What's more, Albert never wanted children and the fact that their only offspring was a girl was a difficult blow. To say that

Ruth and Albert were not well-suited would be an understatement.

Ruth's mom would often overhear Albert telling Ruth how he wished she was more like his previous fiancée, Jessie Guischard, who passed away before they were to be married. If only Ruth could be more serious like her.

Ruth's mother advised her to seek a divorce, instead, Ruth sought a lover.

A tall, blonde woman with a captivating personality, it wasn't hard for Ruth to find a beau. She met a married, corset salesman named Henry Judd Gray at lunch one day. Another man her polar opposite, Henry was short, unremarkable, and quiet. Yet the pair got along fabulously and soon took up a passionate affair.

Albert worked at the magazine during the day and Lorraine, now nine, was in school. On the unfortunate occasions when Lorraine had a holiday, Ruth would leave her in a hotel lobby and sneak to a room upstairs with Henry. The couple was insatiable.

It is hard to say exactly when Ruth crossed from madly in love with another man to murderous. She was bored in her life, and she fought frequently with her husband. Maybe she was looking for excitement and a thrill. Maybe she saw a clear path out of a broken marriage, a plan too fail-proof to pass up. Whatever the case, she probably should've heeded her mother's advice about legally ending her marriage before turning to murder.

Murder for Momsie?

Ruth and Henry had pet names for each other; he was called "Lover Boy" and she "Momsie." When Ruth had made up her mind that her husband had to go, she began to work on warming Henry up to the idea of murder.

At first, she started with hints that Albert mistreated her, then she resorted to persistently nagging him and suggesting that he help her commit the crime. She slowly wore Henry down, though he was so adverse to the idea he took to drinking heavily.

When Ruth had resorted to begging, threatening, and finally demanding that Henry commit murder for Momsie, he gave in. The pair devised a plan.

Ruthless Ruth

Henry would take the train from Syracuse to New York, then he would hop a bus to Long Island and finally arrive in Queens. Henry's old pal, Haddon Gray, agreed to assist with an alibi under the pretense that Henry was going to visit a girlfriend.

In order to dupe Henry's wife, Haddon posted two letters to her in Henry's name, mussed his hotel bed sheets, and hung a "Do Not Disturb" sign on his door. As far as anyone knew, Henry was still in Syracuse. However, he was up to something much more sinister than visiting a girlfriend a few towns over.

On Saturday, March 19, 1927, witnesses would recall that Henry seemingly wanted to be caught. He was spotted walking around Ruth's neighborhood, drinking from a flask in broad daylight; begging for prohibition police to arrest him before he could carry out his lover's dark deed.

But alas he wasn't arrested, at least not yet. He quietly slipped into Ruth's unoccupied home and waited in a spare room for the family to return from a party. Ruth had stocked the room with all the homicidal necessities: a window weight, rubber gloves, and chloroform.

When the family returned around two in the morning, Albert and the couple's daughter quickly retired. Ruth went to visit "Lover Boy" for one last romp before they carried out their nefarious plan. After nearly an hour, the pair snuck into the master bedroom, Henry carrying the window sash weight.

When they arrived they found Albert sleeping deeply, his form completely covered by the blankets. Ruth stood on one side of the bed and Henry on the other. Henry raised the window weight, preparing to bring it down on the unsuspecting husband's head.

Whether it was subconscious reluctance or lack of experience, the weight merely glanced off Albert's skull. Enough to wake him but not do any real damage. He arose from the bed stunned but enraged, furiously trying to fight off his attacker.

Timid and terrified Henry shouted, "Momsie, Momsie, for God's sake, help!" Ruth was unphased. She let out a grunt of disgust, realizing her lover was too weak to finish the deed and she would have to take matters into her own hands.

With steady fists she swiftly seized the weight and bludgeoned her husband's skull, killing him almost instantly. But just to be sure, the pair shoved chloroform-soaked cotton balls up his nose and strangled him with picture frame wire.

That's where the couple's plan ended. What did they do now? With Ruth's daughter Lorraine blissfully unaware of the recent events, she and Henry went downstairs for a nightcap and to discuss the missing details of their plan.

They decided to stage a robbery. They scattered some papers here, flipped over a few chairs there, and finally hid a few objects that Ruth would later claim as stolen. Henry then loosely bound Ruth's hands and feet and slipped away into the night.

Lorraine was awoken by her mother, tied at the wrists and ankles, banging on her door. She ran to the neighbors to phone the police.

A Bad Breakup

The police were suspicious from the beginning, especially because the gruesomeness of Albert's murder wasn't consistent with typical break-ins. None of the signs pointed to robbery, and the most damning evidence was the fact that all of the items Ruth claimed were stolen, the police were able to locate in the Snyder residence. Her missing jewelry was recovered from under her very own mattress.

They turned up Ruth's address book with the names of twenty-eight men, the window weight used to bludgeon Albert was found in the basement, and finally in the master bedroom a small pin. It was emblazoned with the initials J.G. for Jessie Guischard.

Albert was never without the token from his former fiancée, but police matched the J.G. to a name in the recovered address book — "Judd Gray." A pin likely dropped by the murderer corresponding to a name in the vengeful wife's address book? An unlikely coincidence.

When the police asked Ruth about Henry Judd Gray she asked, "Has he confessed?" Yes, he had the police told her. For reasons unknown, Ruth told the truth or at least a half-truth. She admitted to conspiring with Henry but claimed it was him who ultimately dealt the death blow.

Henry was found just a few short hours later, holed up in his hotel room. He put up a bit more of a front than Ruth, asserting his innocence and saying he was nowhere near the city. Until police presented the train ticket stub found in his hotel trash can. He confessed, blaming the whole messy murder on Ruth.

The final nail in the coffin for the pair was a double-indemnity insurance policy Ruth had taken out in Albert's name for nearly one hundred thousand dollars in the event of his accidental death, just before his grisly murder.

The Dumbbell Murder Case

By the time the trial arrived for Henry and Ruth, the former lovers were more than spiteful. They each had separate lawyers proclaiming their innocence and declaring the guilt of the other. While sensational, the trial became known as the dumbbell murder case, for how dumb the whole poorly planned homicide was.

Henry claimed Ruth hypnotized and seduced him, convincing him to murder her abusive husband. Ruth stated that Albert "drove love out of the house" and that Henry assisted her in setting up the insurance policy to tempt her. In fact, Henry regularly took her to speakeasies, tried to convince her to smoke, and even once sent her poison to murder her husband. Henry was the bad influence while she was a pious homemaker, reading the Bible to her daughter and attending church on Sundays.

The media had a field day. Celebrities attended the trial, famous reporters worked overtime, and the authorities and medical coroners were running back and forth testifying in both ongoing trials. The ordeal became one of the top media events of the 1920s. The adultery and subsequent murder proclaimed a "cancer in the city" that was the epitome of many immoral behaviors taking place as of late.

The two former lovers would be made an example and authorities stated, they would "excise this social cancer and re-establish the old standards." The tabloids took a different stance; detailing every forbidden touch, meeting, and behavior. This allowed the public to indulge in a buffet of voyeurism.

By the end of the trial, two things were apparent: the masses couldn't get enough of the thought of sneaking away to a hotel for a mid-day hour of clandestine sex and respectable women did not smoke, drink, dye their hair, cross their legs, lunch out with strange men, or feel ingratitude toward their husbands.

Ruth and Henry may appear ordinary, but they were not, said the authorities. By the end of the trial, Ruth had been made out to be barely a human, much less a lady. She was referred to as "The Granite Woman," "Vampire Wife," or "Ruthless Ruth."

This may have made it easier for the jury to deliver their verdict; Ruth was declared guilty and was sentenced to death by electrocution And Henry? He was just a "poor boob" duped by a woman and unable to stand up for his morals. He received a guilty verdict as well, receiving the same fate as his ex-lover.

Henry and Ruth were executed on the same day, January 12, 1928.

Henry was executed first. Witnesses said he was calm and of a clear conscience, having received a letter of forgiveness from his wife.

Ruth was electrocuted moments later. Her final thoughts making it clear she had learned the lesson the public so desperately wanted to teach her. She said, "If I were to live over again, I would be what I want my child to be—a good girl, really making the fear of God a guide to a straight life."

II

Henry Moity

NEW ORLEANS, 1927. THE CITY WAS IN ITS heyday amidst the roaring twenties. The French Quarter was populated by artists, writers, and performers, fostering a vibrant scene of culture and a little good natured chaos.

Its old-world French charm drew in bohemian lovers from across the globe. Its low-rent costs and proximity to plentiful work opportunities didn't hurt either. While uptown and the suburban edges of the Quarter housed wealthier residents, the heart of the city was strictly middleclass.

It was a culturally diverse community but tended to be home to a large number of Sicilians who had immigrated in the 1880s. They worked hard at the sugar cane factories and warehouses, but enjoyed the liveliness of the city during their time off.

As colorful and flashy as the city was, it wasn't without its darker moments. One such event was a gruesome homicide that appalled and shocked residents, known as the "New Orleans Trunk Murders."

A Startling Discovery

It was a warm fall afternoon on October 27, 1927, when housekeeper Nettie Compass set out to clean a neighboring apartment. Henry and Theresa Moity, along with their three children lived on the second floor of 715 Ursulines Street. A quaint but sturdy building in the heart of the French Quarter.

Henry and Theresa's marriage had seemed to be on the rocks lately, or at least since Theresa's sister, Leonide, moved in with the couple. The women frequently entertained while their husbands were away. Their parenting and homemaking skills often left a lot to be desired.

Nettie had planned to do some light tidying up but she wouldn't make it more than a few steps inside the apartment. She screamed and fled after encountering obvious traces of blood. Her shrieks were overheard by two nearby men who quickly called the police.

The responding officers encountered horrors beyond belief. Mattresses soaked in blood and a bathroom splattered in red hinted at play most foul;severed fingers, like a morbid trail of breadcrumbs, led to two traveling trunks.

At the rear of the apartment sat a tightly sealed trunk, surrounded by walls also splattered with crimson drops. In the front bedroom lay its twin.

When investigators opened the trunks they were confronted with the full horror of the crime. Each trunk contained the corpse of a young woman. Or what was left of them.

The victims had been carefully butchered and expertly packed. Decapitated, their fingers removed, and their arms and legs severed. Orleans Parish Coroner Dr. George Roeling was called in to determine the true cause of death. Were the women alive when they were relieved of their fingers? Were they tortured?

The coroner determined that both women were knocked unconscious with a lead billy club prior to being chopped up with a machete.

Clothing scattered around the apartment amongst the bloody human remains provided little insight into who the women were. The trunks were likely emptied hastily in order to stuff in the bodies.

The murder weapon was discovered to be a sugar-cane knife with a two-foot blade, stashed below disembodied arms and legs in one of the containers. A common tool that any factory worker at one of the Quarters various sugar refineries would possess.

But upon closer inspection the coroner discovered a clue: buried deep in a gash in one of the victim's back was a gold wedding band. The victims were none other than Theresa Moity and her sister Leonide.

The Moity's

Two hours away from the murder scene was New Iberia. The melting-pot city was where Theresa and Leonide previously lived and met their husbands, brothers Henry and Joseph Moity.

Joseph was five years Leonide's senior, and his younger brother Henry was older than his wife by about four years. The sisters married the brothers and both moved from sleepy New Iberia to the bustling French Quarter.

Henry gave up his career as a butcher to become a sign painter while Joseph found work in one of the various factories. The couples settled near to one another, started families, and went about their daily lives.

This idyllic lifestyle seemed ideal for most, until brewing unsatisfaction reared its ugly head. One day, Leonide decided to stray from the routine. Two weeks before she was found dismembered, Joseph returned home from work only to find his wife embracing another man. The brazen Leonide told Joseph to get out, and he did.

He returned home to his family in New Iberia with his daughter and son. Whether he was ashamed, simply fed up with Leonide's antics, or knew his family would be better off without his wayward wife remains unknown.

Unfortunately, his marriage wouldn't be the only one shattered by Leonide. Unable to pay for her home on her own, she went to live with her sister and brother-in-law, Theresa and Henry Moity.

Perhaps Leonide pushed her sister into adultery, or maybe Leonide's split from her husband gave Theresa the courage to do the same. Therese succumbed to her sister's antics; both ladies turned Theresa's home into a revolving door of men when Henry was away.

One man in particular attracted Theresa's attention; and that was Joseph Caruso, the couple's landlord. She wasn't shy about her new fling, flaunting him around town. The two were even spotted holding hands as they strolled carelessly along the city streets.

After the murders, the newspapers had a field day with this information. Highlights proclaiming their "careless parenting" and various infidelities covered the front page. Neighbors fueled the fire, reporting blistering fights about money, accusations of adultery, and frequent drinking.

A blood-stained rejection slip from an editor of a popular women's publication was found at the site of the murder. It corresponded to what is believed to be a thinly-veiled autobiographical account, hidden in Leonide's cabinet.

The writing spun a cautionary tale to young girls about the resolution of matrimony and how to find joy after a failed marriage. *Be careful, for marriage is a life sentence*, read the manuscript.

Husband on the run

As in any murder, the police first turned suspicion on those nearest to the victims. In this case, it was the women's husbands. One of the men in particular was of interest to the police: Henry.

The murderer was clearly adept at using a blade, having chopped up the bodies so expertly. Maybe he had experience processing animals or working in the meatpacking industry, the officers offered.

A quick search into Henry's past revealed he had previously worked as a butcher and was known as a "handy man with a knife." The coroner corroborated, "The killer who decapitated Mrs. Henry Moity… knew enough not to try to cut through the bone, but to cut through the joint. The appearance of the head of the wife of the defendant… indicated that it had been skillfully removed."

Thomas Healey, New Orleans Superintendent of Police, determined the first order of business was finding the husbands.

The city was on high alert. The discovery of a body, sliced and shoved in a trunk was a shock. But the fact that there were two, belonging to young women with husbands and children had citizens reeling.

Joseph, living with his sister only a few hours away, promptly turned himself in and informed police of his separation from his wife after finding her with another man. One husband down, one to go. Henry could not be located and did not seem as likely to hand himself over to authorities.

The last sighting of Henry had been at a Camp Street boarding house. Other occupants reported him talking about travel and making a voyage. He planned to escape by ship. Seven vessels were to depart New Orleans over the next seven days.

Healey informed the captains to keep an eye out for a man with "dark bushy hair, very dark brown eyes, and a tattoo of a naked lady on his arm." Two days after the housekeeper stumbled upon the bloody scene police boarded a freighter named the Gem.

They apprehended Henry who had used a false name to obtain passage. However, the nude lady inked on his arm was a dead giveaway. Henry was taken into the Lafourche Parish Sheriff's office.

Confession and Contempt

The police had Henry's confession in hand within twenty-four hours.

On the afternoon of the murder, Theresa said she was going out with Leonide. Henry would need to stay home and watch the children. The couple fought; the housekeeper Nettie recalls Henry telling her he should just "take a pistol and shoot both of those bastards."

It isn't clear where the women and children went from there, but Henry went bar hopping for most of the afternoon.

He claimed too much alcohol warped his sensibilities and he found himself stopping to buy a knife on the way home. Replaying his wife's infidelities and abandonment of their children over and over in his head, he became obsessed with the possibility that his wife was planning to leave him for good.

He staggered into his home early in the evening. Theresa and Leonide appeared shortly thereafter, and the entire family went out to dinner. It was then that Nettie saw the two women, Henry, and the children leaving the house, all appearing to be in good spirits. On the way out Henry quietly mentioned to Nettie, don't be alarmed if "her family heard the children crying in the early morning."

As the family was out and about, a local gossip made a comment to Theresa. The rumor mills were churning, and the news was that she was going to run away with Joseph Caruso that very night. The flippant comment may have been the final nail in Teresa's coffin; it was the last straw for Henry.

Theresa and Leonide tucked in their children and then went to bed themselves. Henry stayed up, the rumors swirling in his head. And then he snapped.

He went into Theresa's bedroom first, stabbing her to death. Henry then turned on his sister-in-law, the source of all the family's problems, and turned the weapon on her. He deftly cut up the bodies, stuffed them into the trunks, and left.

Henry's retelling of the entire sordid tale ended with this, "If I ever get my hands on that Joe Caruso, I'll chop him up into little pieces, not big pieces like my wife, but little pieces, I'll make him look like something that's been run through a sausage mill… Joe Caruso took my wife. She was beautiful. And I loved her."

Husband on Trial

Henry was tried separately for both murders. The prosecution claimed that this wasn't the work of a maniac, as the defense psychiatrists testified, but a drunk and jealous husband.

Still, the jury couldn't deny the ways of his wandering wife. Though they found him guilty of both counts, they pleaded with the judge for mercy. Henry wouldn't be hung, instead he would serve two life sentences.

But Henry's tale doesn't end there. On July 6, 1928, he became Convict #18038 at the Louisiana State Penitentiary. Despite being found guilty of slicing up two people and shoving their bodies in trunks he was given an astounding number of special freedoms within the jail. He wasn't heavily guarded and was permitted to run errands for the prison personnel outside the barbed wire gates.

Sixteen years after he began his sentence, Henry skipped town. During a routine trip to the post office the inmate hailed a taxi then boarded the Illinois Central Panama Limited en route to Chicago. The warden was shockingly unphased. Henry would soon return of his own volition he claimed, after all he was near to being pardoned on the grounds of temporary insanity induced by alcohol.

Henry didn't return. The trunk murderer of the French Quarter enjoyed two years of freedom until police in St. Louis, Missouri, rounded him up in 1946 for suspicious behavior and shipped him back to Louisiana.

Although Henry was returned to jail, he wouldn't be an inmate for long. Two charges for murder and two years on the lam weren't enough to deny his pardon. On March 26, 1948, the governor of Louisiana signed off on Henry's freedom.

The former sign painter was determined to start anew, he moved to California to find a job in his previous line of work. Almost thirty years after brutally murdering his wife and sister-in-law, Henry's rage boiled over again.

In January 1956, thirty-five-year-old Alberta Orange, rang the front desk of her LA hotel. "I've been shot!" she shrieked. The attacker? None other than her husband, Henry Moity.

The couple was allegedly arguing after Alberta asked him for money for clothes. He shot her in the chest, puncturing her lung. Henry was again on the stand, this time only for attempted murder and assault with a deadly weapon. A charge that pales in comparison to his former crimes.

He received five years at Folsom Prison. This time Mr. Moity wouldn't live to gain his freedom and kill again.

In 1957, he died of a stroke, one year into his sentence. Henry Moity desperately tried to live an honest and normal life, but circumstances and his choices turned him into someone he never intended to be – The New Orleans Trunk Murderer.

III

Nannie Doss

IF YOU WERE CONTEMPLATING MARRIAGE, THE first two tales may have dampened your spirits. But be warned, this next story will likely put you off the idea of matrimony for good.

It is proof that serial killers come in all shapes and sizes. Your neighbor? The sweet elderly lady from church? You never know. The residents of Tulsa, Oklahoma, would have never guessed that the jovial grandma who they waved to on the street and passed in the supermarket aisle was actually a cold-hearted murderess.

By the time her serial killing spree ended she had almost wiped out half her family tree. For over thirty years Nannie Doss, later known by monikers such as "The Jolly Black Widow," single-handedly killed off relatives in the pursuit of true love.

The Giggling Grandma

Unfortunately, Nannie wasn't always so cheerful. Her upbringing in Blue Mountain, Alabama, was tough. Ruled over by a hard, unloving father, she and her four siblings stayed home most days to do chores and farm labor instead of attending school.

She dropped out of the education system after the sixth grade. Her parents, James Hazel and Louisa Holder, had little interest in having her attend.

For Nannie, a head injury she received while riding on a train at the age of seven, made it difficult to concentrate on things. As a result of the accident, Nannie experienced migraines, blackouts, and depression. This coupled with numerous accounts of molestation as a child would deeply affect her for the rest of her life.

When Nannie was a teen, she dreamed of escaping the abuse of her father and life on the small family farm. She adored reading the "lonely hearts" columns of magazines, dreaming of her future husband and a quaint neighborhood far away.

She wouldn't have to wait long to meet Mr. Right. He appeared in the form of a co-worker, Charley Braggs. At work he was kind and Nannie appreciated the sweet way he took care of his unmarried mother. In just five short months, the couple went from dating to married. Nannie moved in with her husband and his mother.

That's when things went downhill for Nannie. Her mother-in-law was controlling and made life torturous. Things weren't any better than they had been on the farm.

Trading Marriage for Murder

In 1923, the couple, Nannie and Charley, had their first daughter. They would have three more girls over the next few years. Her husband rarely came home and began having affairs. Charley was drinking constantly and was becoming abusive. Nannie's life was dominated by the demands of her mother-in-law and her children. She turned to drinking and was suspected of affairs, too. The marriage began to crumble.

When Charley was around, he became disturbed by his children's behavior. They seemed healthy when he left in the morning but would often be ill by dinner. Each time he went to leave they cried and begged him to stay. One day, Charley went to work and when he got home that night, he was informed that his two middle daughters had died in convulsions at the breakfast table.

People didn't often die of food poisoning. Not so quickly, and not when none of the other family members were affected. Charley strongly believed Nannie poisoned their daughters. A few months after the deaths he fled with the couple's oldest daughter, Melvina. He left their newborn, Florine, and his own mother to fend for themselves with his possibly murderous wife.

Not long after, Charley's mother passed away, and with her no longer owning the home Charley returned with his girlfriend and Melvina. He divorced Nannie; she and her two daughters were forced to move back in with her parents. Charley would turn out to be the luckiest of the men in Nannie's life.

Living with her parents and working a mundane job, Nannie was eager to get back into wedded bliss. She scoured the "Lonely Hearts" column, where men advertised looking for love. In her prime, Nanny was quite attractive; though it was her girlish giggle that really enticed her suitors. She wrote to many of them, but only one returned her affections.

Robert (Frank) Harrelson, a factory worker, was only twenty-three when he met Nannie in 1929.. She was now twenty-four and had been divorced for two years. He wrote her poems and she baked him cakes. The infatuated couple was soon wed. A few months into their whirlwind relationship, Nannie would come to learn that Frank had a criminal record for assault and was an alcoholic.

Gruesome Grandma

Nannie stayed in the marriage for reasons unknown. She preoccupied herself with the impending birth of her first grandchild. In 1943, Nannie's oldest daughter Melvina gave birth. Nannie was by her daughter's side to offer her help, and quickly took the child after Melvina's difficult labor.

The baby didn't stay long in this world, dying a few short hours later. Nannie, the doting new grandma, nonchalantly informed the couple that their child was dead.

Melvina would later state how in her weakened state she thought she had seen Nannie stick a hatpin into the child's head, likely piercing the brain. Her husband also recalled seeing Nannie holding the pin. The doctors could not explain the infant's death.

Melvina and her husband split after the shocking passing of their firstborn. Melvina began a relationship with a soldier. Nannie disapproved of her beau, and they fought constantly.

On July 7, 1945, Nannie was fuming after a particularly nasty argument. Melvina went to visit her father, leaving her two-year-old son in his grandma's care. When she went to pick him up, he was dead. Doctors later declared it was death by asphyxiation from unknown causes. Two months after the death, the grieving grandma collected a five hundred dollar life insurance policy she had taken out on the child.

Racking up the Body Count

Nannie quickly realized how easy life could be, doing away with those that bothered her and even making a little money in the process. No longer would she be dominated by other members of her family; she was in control – or so she thought.

After a drunken night of celebration spurred by the ending of WW2, her husband Frank raped her. The next morning Nannie discovered her husband's hidden jar of corn whiskey buried in the garden. She added a healthy dose of rat poison. Frank suffered an excruciating death on September 15, 1945.

Nannie quickly renewed her membership to the "Lonely Hearts" column club, combing the advertisements at every opportunity. Within a few days of meeting Arlie Lanning of North Carolina, Nannie said "I do" at the altar. However, Nannie seemed to have bad luck with men, for she soon found out that Arlie was a drunk and a womanizer.

Nannie couldn't risk suspicion. She played the picture-perfect housewife, doting on her husband while secretly biding her time. Two and a half years after they were married, Arlie died. The entire town came out to support his loving wife Nannie at the funeral. Doctors believed the poor woman's husband suffered heart failure after the flu, his system weakened by years of abusing the bottle. An autopsy was never performed.

After Arlie was six feet under, Nannie discovered he left their home to his sister, and not long after, the house burned to the ground in a fire. With a lump sum of insurance money in her account, Nannie left town to go live with her sister, but not before Arlie's mother was pronounced dead in her sleep. With a bag and body count mounting, Nannie arrived at her sister, Dovie's home.

Ailing and ill, Dovie was bedridden. Nannie swooped in to tend to her kin. But her duty was sweet and short, for soon after her arrival, her sister died. Three family members down, and now husbandless, Nannie needed something or someone to preoccupy her time.

She became a member of the Diamond Circle Club where she met husband number four Richard Morton of Emporia, Kansas. He wasn't an alcoholic, but he did possess one of the traits of his predecessors: a womanizer.

For a while, Nannie wasn't wise to his adultery. She was caring for her mother, Louisa, who broke a hip in 1953. Louisa wouldn't need Nannie's services for long though, she died just a few months after her daughter moved in. As did one of Nannie's sisters, very unexpectedly.

With time on her hands, Nannie returned home, only to learn of her husband's extramarital affairs. Three months later, Richard was dead.

Nannie was back on the market. In June 1953, she met Samuel Doss, of Tulsa, Oklahoma. Nanny may have been a grandma now, in status as well as looks, but she still knew how to turn on the charm with her giggle.

It seemed that Nannie finally met the man she had been searching for her entire life. Samuel never touched alcohol, was a God-fearing man, and wouldn't run around with other women.

He didn't even cuss. He counted his blessings when he met Nannie; she was a good cook and good natured woman, he believed she would keep him happy until death did them part.

Till death do us part arrived sooner than Samuel thought. Nannie was jolly, and a whiz in the kitchen when she wasn't cooking with rat poisoning, but there was something that she was not; strictly conservative. It was on this topic that Sam would make his fatal mistake.

He set a strict routine, for bed, for sex, even for when lights were allowed to be turned on and off in the couple's home. Books, radio, and all forms of entertainment were to be educational in nature only.

"Christian women don't need television or romance magazines to be happy!" Sam told Nannie. He wanted to take away her newspapers, her "Lonely Hearts" columns, her magazines that had been a form of escapism since she was a small child.

Nannie needed a break. She set out to Alabama to mull over her options. As soon as she left her husband forwarded letters, begging for her to come back. Nannie would only agree on one condition: end his overbearing ways.

To prove it, Sam let her spend money more freely; ultimately moving all their finances to a shared bank account and naming Nannie beneficiary of both his life insurance policies. That was all Nannie needed to seal the deal, not for a happy marriage but murder.

In September, Nannie lovingly served her husband his favorite prune cake. But soon he was in excruciating pain. Convulsing, retching, plagued by spasms he was bedridden for days, eventually losing so much weight his doctor had him transported to the hospital.

When he was released the next month, having recovered from a "severe infection to the digestive tract," Nannie was there to welcome him home. She served him a cup of coffee as a precursor to an extravagant pot roast she had whipped up in celebration. The pot roast was delicious and free from poison. The same could not be said for the coffee.

That night, Samuel Doss died. The attending doctor at the hospital couldn't believe his healthy-again patient died so soon after his release. He ordered an autopsy. Nannie had been too eager to make up for time missed while Sam was in the hospital. She erred and the autopsy would unravel her whole terrifying tale.

It returned unbelievable levels of arsenic in Sam's body. Mixed with pot roast his intestines contained enough poison to take down a "team of horses." Nannie had no explanation. While the authorities had dismissed the deaths of her previous nine family members, this one would not be swept under the rug.

The Black Widow Confesses

Nannie was not very forthcoming in her involvement in Sam's poisoning. She denied having any knowledge of the poison, his illness, and his subsequent death. The police did not let up, reminding her that arsenic isn't a naturally occurring chemical in a pot roast. She giggled at their assumptions, why would she want to poison her doting husband?

"Why would you want to kill any of your husbands, Ms. Doss," asked Special Agent Ray Page. "We're putting two and two together, Nannie, and it looks like we just might come up with... well, four. Arsenic, Nannie, we believe that they all died of arsenic."

Nannie confessed to killing four of her five husbands. She said that they either annoyed her, made her mad, or were drinking and shining up to other women. "Now my conscience is clear," said Nannie.

The coroner set to work exhuming some of the bodies, and in each, they found high concentrations of arsenic or rat poison. From the time of her arrest to her confession, word had spread that she was being held on suspicion of murder. The police station phone began ringing off the hook with reports of other people who had died after being close to Nannie.

Her first husband, Charley Braggs is known as "the one that got away." Police interviewed him and he said that the whole family was afraid of Nannie, and they knew better than to eat or drink anything she prepared when she was in a bad mood. Police learned that unfortunately, their two young daughters did not survive their mother's wrath; and the daughters that did survive would produce granddaughters who met the same fate as their deceased aunts.

Nannie had confessed to four murders, at least eight more were under investigation. Her mother and sister, possibly her father; the list went on. Could there be others who had crossed Nannie's path only to annoy her and not make it to the other side? Eventually, Nannie confessed to killing her mother, her sister, her grandson, and her mother-in-law in addition to four husbands.

She seemed to revel in the limelight of her arrest, being called "Arsenic Annie" and the "Black Widow." She would crack jokes about her "worthless" dead husbands and detail the methods she used to kill them. Investigators wondered whether her guileless murders were a result of her head injury and traumatic upbringing, but the jury found her mentally fit for trial.

Nannie maintained that she wasn't crazy and that her murders were not motivated by money. Instead, it was something purer that drove her to kill. "I was searching for the perfect mate, the real romance of life," she said. Unfortunately, that didn't tell the jury why she ruthlessly killed her innocent grandchildren.

Nanny pleaded guilty to her crimes on May 17, 1955, receiving a life sentence. After three decades and at least ten murders, Nannie was behind bars. Dating clubs and columns were once again safe, but prospective husbands be warned, watch out for a scorned woman.

Ultimately, the Lonely Hearts Serial Killer would not die of a broken heart, but leukemia ten years later in 1965.

IV

Paul Pappas

BEFORE WE BEGIN OUR DISSECTION OF THE "lady in the ashes" case, a few notes about life in the 1920s. During those days the dust and debris from city streets and sidewalks were copious and referred to as ash. Windows, gates, and doors weren't insulated or sealed well, and this led to the dirt easily permeating homes, especially basements whose windows were positioned at street level or below.

The ash buildup would collect on basement floors and become damp then dry with the changing seasons, and over time it would compress. Basement floors often resembled a cross between compost and paper mâché.

It was within a pile of ashes, left to rot in a basement, that a body would be discovered. The body of a woman who had been missing for four months. The story of how she got there is twisted and strange. An argument with her tenant, a web of lies, and of course murder.

Jealousy Gone too far

Mrs. Alice Arsenault and her husband owned a lodging house in Boston during the early 1900s. The city was full of life and bustling residents gave it a sense of vitality. Many people flooded into the metropolis to work and live. Immigrants and citizens alike often needed a place to stay, most of them turned to lodging houses, like the tall brick building owned by Mrs. Arsenault at 517 Columbus Avenue.

Paul Dascalakis, or Paul Pappas as he was known, was a lodger. He arrived on the steps of Mrs. Arsenault's building in September of 1919. From that time on, Paul and Alice had a "friendly intimacy" that was casually observed by her other lodgers. But Alice wasn't committed to Paul, at least not in the way he was committed to her.

She was a woman of the 1920s and felt empowered to express herself and follow her ambitions. She entertained other men now and again in addition to Paul and her husband. One of these fellows was Arthur Pelletier, who would come to call on her from time to time. Paul hated Arthur.

When he saw the couple together, a jealous rage came over him. Once he happened upon Arthur and Alice in a room with the door closed. One could only guess at what was happening away from prying eyes. Paul was enraged, quoted as saying, "someday he would get mad and kill both Pelletier and Alice Arsenault."

Christmas day Disappearance

Just a few short months after Paul began renting a room from Alice, the weather turned chilly. The fall faded into winter and Christmas day was quickly approaching. Perhaps Paul had expected a token of Alice's affection as a present, or maybe he had hoped to express his undying love during that cheerful holiday season. Perhaps no one will ever know, but what we do know is that he witnessed Alice giving a gift to someone else.

This would be his tipping point. Paul was overcome with envy that Alice would celebrate the holiday with someone else, giving that person a special present and leaving him out in the cold. Christmas Day 1919 would be the last time anyone remembered seeing Alice Arsenault alive.

As the holiday festivities carried on, the lodgers began to worry. Where was their landlord? Who would care for the building, collect the rent, and allow them a place to live? On January 7, a bill of sale appeared with Alice's signature. The furniture of the lodging house had been sold off for eight hundred seventy-five dollars.

Legal documents also bore Alice's signature. The home was sold for eight hundred dollars. Paul Pappas knew where Mrs. Arsenault was. She had left her husband for good, he said, she was hiding out in Springfield, Massachusetts, until she could get a divorce.

While things may have not added up for the renters, one thing was clear, they needed to find somewhere else to live. Lodging houses were a dime a dozen, and the house was eventually cleared out. The newspapers of the time don't make it evident where Alice's husband was during all of this or why he wasn't concerned with his wife's disappearance. Perhaps he too entertained women on the side and with Alice out of the picture, he was free to do as he pleased.

Paul no longer had a room in the home either and like the other lodgers, had moved away. He eventually settled in Montreal, Canada.

The Lady in the Ashes

Four months after Alice's disappearance, a new owner moved into the home. By this time, it was in a state of disrepair, especially the basement. The ashes had not been shoveled all winter and they were built up in a thick layer. In May, ash-men were called in to clean up the mess. While shoveling the heavy debris into an ash can, they made a startling discovery.

There in the damp grey grit was a body. The remains belonged to Alice Arsenault. Her throat had been slit from ear to ear and her chalky corpse was covered in stab wounds. She had also been stripped of her jewelry, including her wedding band.

Police began to look into Mrs. Arsenault's former acquaintances and lodgers. Most were still in the area and recalled seeing their landlord for the last time on Christmas Day 1919. They described how the building was quickly cleaned out and sold.

One lodger was especially difficult to track down, Paul Pappas. In their search police also discovered that he and Alice had a history that extended beyond their friendly intimacy while he was a boarder in her home. The pair knew each other for a little over a year when they each lived in Revere, Massachusetts.

Determined to find their man, they finally caught up with Paul and apprehended him in Montreal in September 1921. When they questioned him and his wife, police noticed her ring looked eerily similar to the one Alice's husband had described.

Paul claimed that he had no idea who killed Alice. The last time he had seen her was Christmas Day, 1919, when she was "in a room with two fellows." Paul detailed how he had moved around the country since then and learned of her death from a newspaper in Akron, Ohio, before finally settling down in Canada.

The ring on Paul's wife's finger belonged to Mrs. Arsenault, as did the cash made from the sale of her home and furniture that Paul had pocketed before he fled.

On June 15, 1922, Paul Pappas was found guilty of murder in a Boston court.

In late June or early July of 1923, he was executed by electric chair. The details surrounding the case have been lost over time, but the lady in the ashes murder captured the public's attention in

Boston and the surrounding states. Though there were many suspicions about Paul's motives, what ultimately drove him to murder was unclear.

His new wife had no knowledge of his wicked past, proving that anyone could have a dark side you know nothing about.

V
The Broadway Butterfly Murders

BROADWAY IN THE 1920S WAS A GLOWING beacon, beckoning people from all walks of life to its glittering theaters and flashing billboards. It wasn't uncommon to find young women, aspiring starlets, drawn to its stages. "Broadway Butterflies" they were called. Like an insect attracted to the light, they held onto the promise of "fame, fortune, and romance."

Equally as plentiful as the delicate actresses were the sugar daddies. Wealthy, jealous, and notoriously rough, they were the polar opposite of the svelte Broadway Butterflies. The term "Sugar Daddy" first became popular in American vocabulary in the spring of 1923. It gained recognition thanks to a New York high society murder.

The maid trudged up the private staircase and let herself into the lavish apartment. Being that her employer was a glamorous companion to doting and wealthy men, she wasn't surprised to find the house quiet. Ms. King often slept late into the afternoon. Yet as she let her gaze sweep across the home, her nerves became unsettled. Ms. King's belongings were strewn about and furniture had been flipped over. Startled by what appeared to be more than the scene of a passionate late-night romp, she rushed to the bedroom. Reaching out to rouse Ms. King, she hurriedly snapped her hand back. The body was cold and her appendages were bent at unnatural angles, while a delicate silk negligee covered the ivory skin of the former Broadway Butterfly.

From Rags to Royalty

Dorothy "Dot" King, born Anna Marie Keenan, grew up in Harlem. Her first-generation Irish immigrant family lived in poverty and Dorothy always knew she wanted something better for herself.

She was a good-looking girl with a petite figure; using this natural charm and beauty to secure a modeling position, she worked her way up and soon found herself modeling clothes in the haute couture shops of Manhattan. It was here that she would get her first taste of fame and notoriety.

Through her gigs, she began to meet the upper echelon of New York society. Kingpins like Arnold Rothstein, businessman, racketeer, and head of the Jewish Mob in NYC; but also scions descended from families of great wealth. The upper crust of the city was a melting pot of old money, nouveau riche, and a handful of individuals who made their money in black market dealings.

Dorothy married a chauffeur, and his proximity to the rich and famous opened doors for her to meet the upper crust members of New York. Unfortunately, the marriage ended in divorce when Dorothy's husband caught her having an affair. But by this point, Dorothy had gained from him what she wanted, entry into some of the most elite circles.

Dorothy's family believed she was a model and actress, having seen her appear in a production called Broadway Brevities of 1920, that ran for one hundred five performances in late 1920. What they didn't know was that the aspiring performer was only catering to a private audience. Dorothy was described as "a lady with more charm than virtue" or what was known as a "vamp" — someone who entertained in their boudoir and often wore tight clothing, red lipstick, and a sultry smile.

She was known in many circles, within speakeasies and clubs, for making small talk with wealthy men and having drinks with powerful gangsters. Dorothy quickly rose to become a popular feature of the New York City social scene. Some of her most famous friends included the son of President Warren Harding's Attorney General and the millionaire son-in-law of Edward T. Stotesbury, one of the wealthiest men in America.

Dorothy's suitors were eager to stake their claim on her and it is estimated she was gifted more than fifteen thousand in jewels and fashions throughout her short career. One, a steel magnate named Albert Guimares, even robbed his own company and then engaged in stock fraud to compete for her affections against other billionaires of the time. Unfortunately, Guimares was also known for giving her bruises and black eyes, yet she still entertained the suave Puerto Rican time and again.

Only one man would win the title of Dorothy's "sugar daddy" — this was Stotesbury's son-in-law J. Kearsley Mitchell.

Sugar Daddy of Death

Mitchell set the bar high for all the other men in her life; he gave her jewels, furs, and clothes. His most expensive gift was a classy apartment right on the edge of Central Park. This may have been more for his benefit than hers though as he was a fifty-year-old married man and viewed as a financial tycoon of the East Coast. It wasn't fitting for him to appear in public with a twenty-year-old vamp on his arm. He visited the apartment frequently to see Dorothy away from prying eyes.

Mitchell was so secretive that he always went to see Dorothy with his lawyer, Mr. Wilson (a moniker). Wilson would make sure the coast was clear and then they would ride up together to her apartment. After exchanging pleasantries, the lawyer would leave, tipping the elevator boy generously for his secrecy.

On the afternoon of March 14, 1923, Mitchell and Wilson made their way up to Dorothy's apartment. She greeted both of them and then breezed into the lavish apartment. She left her maid to receive a bouquet of flowers adorned with a diamond and jade bracelet on her behalf.

Mitchell and Dorothy had a short evening out and then returned to her home around midnight; the maid and Mr. Wilson had long since taken their leave. Mr. Mitchell departed Dorothy's residence around two thirty in the morning by way of the elevator.

The next morning the maid used the private staircase and let herself into Dorothy's apartment. Though it was after eleven in the morning it wasn't uncommon for the Broadway Butterfly to be still sleeping off the night's affairs. What was odd was the state of the apartment. Pictures were tossed around the room and drawers ransacked. The maid hurriedly went in to wake her, only to find Dorothy dead in her bed; dressed in a skimpy, silky negligee.

Despite the state of the apartment, police first suspected suicide. However, when the coroner arrived, he noted the unnatural appearance of Dorothy's body. Her legs curled beneath her and the bruises surrounding her neck. Upon further investigation, the bedsheets were found to be harboring the murder weapon and a bottle of chloroform.

They did not turn up any cotton or gauze that would indicate Dorothy had dosed herself; besides, the chemical is nearly impossible to commit suicide with. The maid clued the police in on two more important discoveries. Dorothy's fifteen thousand dollars in jewels were gone along with her letters from her Sugar Daddy, J. Kearsley Mitchell. The maid informed police that

Mitchell and Albert Guimares were the only people Dorothy ever let into her apartment.

Blackmail or Robbery

Police estimated the murder had occurred around six in the morning. No sooner did they pronounce her murdered as a result of either robbery or blackmail, did the newspapers start running the headline: *Broadway butterfly, Dorothy King, dead in bed with her jewels gone.*

Mitchell and the "Broadway Jackal" Albert Guimares topped the police's suspect list. Mitchell quickly turned himself in and admitted to having been with Dorothy until around two the previous morning. The elevator operator confirmed seeing him leave. Within a few hours, his alibi was deemed valid and Mitchell was cleared of murder.

Next, they brought in Guimares, who was known for having a temper and being a jealous lover. Though a friend of Dorothy's told police she had recently confided in her that she was seeking charges against Guimares for threats and abuse, the steel magnate's alibi was airtight.

Two witnesses vouched for his whereabouts the morning of the murder. Police made a statement that Guimares was confirmed to be with Edmund McBrien and "an attractive blonde" during the time Dorothy was being chloroformed and strangled. Investigators strongly suspected Guimares involvement, but they were not able to prosecute him.

The case went cold. For six years police followed up the occasional lead until they truly hit a dead end. Aurelia Fischer Dreyfus, the "attractive blonde," turned out to be Edward McBrien's girlfriend who testified she was with Guimares the night Dorothy died. Six years after the murder Aurelia sustained fatal injuries when she either fell or was pushed from a yacht balcony where she had been partying with McBrien.

Before she succumbed at a local hospital, she had this admission according to her sister and mother, "I perjured myself in the Dot King murder." Still, police were not able to charge Guimares.

Mr. Mitchell made amends with his wife and did not make headlines again until his death at age seventy-eight.

Guimares changed his name to Santos after he was found guilty of stock fraud and served three years in prison. Upon his release and subsequent name change, he faded into obscurity, dying in 1952.

The Murder of the Broadway Butterfly remains unsolved. Was it actually her sugar daddy J. Kearsley Mitchell, who was too wealthy and too powerful to be touched by law enforcement? Or was it Guimares, the jealous Broadway Jackal, who had been scorned by his lover one too many times?

Another Butterfly Falls

A year after Dorothy's death another murder of an aspiring starlet turned sugar baby would bring the Broadway Butterfly murder to the forefront of everyone's minds.

Like Dorothy, the slain Lou Lawson had traded Broadway for wealthy beaus. Her lover was Gerhardt H. Dahl, chairman of the executive committee of the BMT. Flush with cash, he provided her an apartment, a five hundred dollar a week allowance, and plenty of expensive gifts.

On Friday, February 8, Lou was discovered by her maid. Tied up with "silken hose and torn slips of filmy underwear," gagged with cloth, and her mouth sealed with surgical tape. Twenty thousand dollars in jewels was missing. On her door was taped a coded message that was deciphered to read: "Louise Lawson is alone so long."

Both Dorothy and Lou frequented the same clubs and were known to belong to a clique of "cabarets habitues." Two theories surfaced for the women's murders. One was that an organized gang set the ladies up, using a female spotter to gain their trust, and then robbed them of jewels, possessions, or anything that could be used for blackmail.

Other ladies said it was a common occurrence.

"The girl seldom squeals," another robbery victim stated. "She's afraid to. If they get her jewels, she tells her friends that she lost or hocked them."

The second theory is much darker but was never really unraveled from New York's upper crust's twisted web of lies, associations, and black-market dealings. "Dot and Lou were always together a lot before Dot was murdered," Hilda Ferguson, another member of the clique, told police. "I always thought that Lou knew much more about Dot's death than she dared tell and that she could have implicated certain people."

To this day, the case of the Murder of the Broadway Butterflies remains unsolved, with the answers as fleeting as the butterflies themselves.

VI
Buried Alive: The Story of Marie Billings

IN THE EARLY 1920S AND 1930S, FEATS OF endurance attracted lots of people. A popular sideshow was being buried alive. Men and women were entombed for minutes, and even hours, in wooden coffins below ground.

One such grave occupant was Marie Billings. Only, she wasn't buried by choice, and she just narrowly escaped a claustrophobic death. Clawing her way to a nearby freeway, dragging a bloody blanket and untethered electrical cord. Marie was desperate to escape her premature resting spot.

LA in the Roaring Twenties

LA in the 1920s became synonymous with Hollywood. Actors, actresses, and those seeking fame fled to the metropolis. In the twenties, the population of Los Angeles more than doubled. There were picturesque gardens, stunning architectural feats, and general beautification of the industrial city.

As individuals flooded into the city, housing prices soared. People were looking for homes and real estate was booming.

Marie and Howard Billings lived just east of Los Angeles, in the suburb of Montebello. Their home sat at 5911 Allston Street, not far from where Howard worked as a manufacturer.

It was a squat ranch, flanked on either side by nearly identical homes. Nothing was especially remarkable about the house; it had a small yard and a white picket fence. What it did not have was a for sale sign staked in the lawn.

That is why, when on May 9, 1928, late in the afternoon, Marie was taken by surprise when a real estate salesman appeared on her porch. He aroused her from her chores with a sharp knock on the door. When she answered, the man loomed over her.

His nearly six foot four frame was clad in a dark grey pinstripe suit. He said he was a local agent and hoped to buy the home. Marie and Howard had no plans of selling, yet ever the respectful and kind lady, Marie figured there was no harm in hearing him out.

After they talked for a few minutes on the porch she invited him in to finish their conversation.

Bludgeoned and Buried

As soon as the pair were inside the house, the man bludgeoned Marie on the head with a club he had concealed in his suit. Marie struggled but it was no use. In the chaos, he tore her clothing before he quickly tied her up with an electrical cord.

Disoriented and helpless, there was little Marie could do to stop the silk stocking from being threaded around her neck. Within a few brief moments, she was choked into unconsciousness.

As soon as Marie was out, the man removed the silk stocking from her neck and used it to gag her. His car, a Ford Coupe, was parked in front of the Billings house.

He wrapped her in a blanket, presumably to hide her from neighbors, and carried her out to his vehicle. Once she was stowed in the backseat he rounded the car, got behind the wheel, and drove away.

Nearly eight miles down the road from where he assaulted Marie in her own home, he pulled over. The area was known as Turnbull Canyon and was located in Whittier. Part of the Puente Hills Preserve, the desolate forest had few trails, thickly wooded areas, and steep drainage ravines. It was now evening and the area was lightly trafficked.

The man dumped Marie out into the dirt, roughly ripping away the blanket. He had only choked her until she passed out. The man bent down to ensure that she still had a pulse, and Marie was indeed alive. He rummaged in his car and returned with an iron bar, beating her until he was sure she must be dead.

Then he covered her presumed lifeless body with dirt, leaves, and brush. He casually strolled to his car and drove off into the night.

Confident that he had beaten Marie to death, the man likely believed that he would get away with his crime. However, sometime later, Marie's eyes fluttered. As she strained to open them, she felt a crushing weight, not only on her eyelids but her entire body.

The rusty smell of blood mixed with damp loamy earth choked Marie, as she inhaled grit and dirt with every breath. She quickly realized she was in her own grave, buried alive and left for dead. Gravely injured, she clawed her way through the debris until she made it to the surface.

Marie then crawled, forcing her beaten and bruised body to make it two hundred yards to the nearest road. The remains of the electrical cord used to restrain her dragged behind her, under one arm she cradled the bloody blanket her attacker had used to carry her to his car.

As she lay by the roadside, her feeble attempts at flagging down a passing car were spotted by a taxi driver named W.J. Collins. He quickly assisted Marie into his vehicle and sped her to the Murphy Memorial Hospital in Whittier.

Upon retelling her strange tale, the Los Angeles County Sheriff's Department was phoned. When she was well enough, Captain William Bright, lead investigator, probed Marie for details on her kidnapping and attempted murder. Marie told investigators everything she remembered and described how her five hundred dollar diamond ring was missing.

Reflecting on her brutal beating and burial, Marie recalled that the man seemed familiar. In fact, she believed the real estate agent had paid her a visit only a year before the attack. One of Marie's neighbors, Mrs. Robert D. Ellis, remembered seeing the man as well. "I saw a man leaving the Billings house two or three days before the attack. He was carrying a large package and got into a Ford Coupe and drove away."

But who was the man, and what did he want? Police wondered. The presumed real estate agent's motive for abducting and attempting to kill Marie remained unclear. There wasn't much evidence, only the restraints, the silk stocking, and the bloody blanket remained, as did the fact that Marie's wedding band was nowhere to be found.

Howard, Marie's husband, was determined to bring the unidentified man to justice. He went to the makeshift grave recently occupied by his wife and found a torn scrap of clothing with a powder-burned hole as if from the bullet of a gun. Upon turning over the evidence to police, the investigators theorized that two men could have been involved.

Perhaps both men were in on the attack and attempted murder together and had quarreled over the ring. One man shot the other and left both him and Marie for dead. Alternatively, maybe a visitor to the preserve noticed the man beating and burying Marie. When he tried to intervene, the real estate agent shot him and buried both bodies.

Police believed another unmarked grave existed somewhere as Marie had no bullet wounds. The police scoured the area and could not find a body, a grave, or any clues to speak of.

Billing's home had produced one piece of evidence, a length of pipe that contained one clear fingerprint. Unfortunately, no match was ever made to identify the owner of the fingerprint.

As both the search for a grave and a suspect were fruitless, the case went cold. To this day the mystery remains. Who was the man and why did he attack Marie? To whom did the clothing with the bullet hole belong? Does Turnbull Canyon contain other unmarked graves hiding bodies abducted and beaten by a sadistic real estate agent?

The case of the woman buried alive remains one of LA's many unsolved crimes.

VII
Leopold and Loeb

THEY THOUGHT THEY COULD PULL OFF THE perfect crime. robbers, murderers, bootleggers; criminals of all sorts have long tried to achieve this feat. In the 1920s, two wealthy university students believed they had concocted a flawless plan.

To prove their intellectual superiority, they would carry out a murder that they believed would have no consequences. The victim was a child, a local fourteen-year-old boy hand-selected by the homicidal geniuses.

The horrible and gruesome event took place overnight, but had been discussed for several months. Leopold and Loeb thought without a doubt they would achieve "the crime of the century."

Fortunate Sons

Leopold and Loeb are commonly referred to as a pair, identified only by their last names. The young men were alike in more ways than one. For starters, they were both geniuses.

Nathan Leopold, sometimes referred to as Leo, grew up in the wealthy Chicago suburbs. His parents were German-Jewish immigrants and provided Leopold with the best education possible.

He was proclaimed to be a child prodigy, having spoken his first words at just four months old. At the time of the murder, he was said to have spoken over fifteen languages. He was on his way to Harvard Law School after completing his undergraduate degree at the University of Chicago. Being a lawyer and a linguist were not his only talents, he was also a nationally renowned ornithologist.

Nathan Leopold and Richard Loeb became fast friends in their teen years. Like Leo, Loeb was incredibly smart. Also Jewish, and extremely wealthy, the pair moved in the same circles. Loeb skipped several grades at the Harvard School for Boys, a preparatory academy. He then went on to become the University of Michigan's youngest graduate at the young age of seventeen.

Leopold and Loeb both spent the days of their youth on Chicago's southside in a ritzy neighborhood known as Kenwood. Their families' mansions resided only two blocks from one another. Leopold was the shy, reserved, and quiet one, where Loeb was his opposite. The brazen teen loved to socialize, play sports, and entertain the opposite sex.

The true bond of their friendship centered on crime. While both were students at the University of Chicago they discovered their passion for Friedrich Nietzsche's concept of supermen. They believed Nietzsche was referring to a class of humans who were so intelligent and extraordinary that they could rise above the laws and the rules that governed the general population. In other words, they thought they were immune to any consequences incurred by committing acts of crime and they soon began to test their theories.

From Minor Robberies to Murder

Leopold and Loeb began committing petty acts of theft, arson, and vandalism. Loeb was admittedly keener on the adventures, often convincing Leopold to be his accomplice. One night in November 1923, the pair had just succeeded in a routine robbery.

They drove Leopold's red sports car from Chicago to Ann Arbor to burglarize Loeb's university fraternity. However, they only managed to procure eighty dollars, a penknife, a typewriter, and a few watches. Loeb was tired of the small rewards and the even smaller state of media attention.

He had been mulling over the idea of the perfect crime, specifically the perfect murder. One that would stump the police, fascinate the public, and prove once and for all that they were the epitome of Nietzsche's supermen.

The trust-fund twins decided that to get Chicago talking, they would need to kidnap and murder a child. Writing a ransom note and demanding money from the parents would make the crime even more sensational. The abduction and death of an innocent child would be so shocking that no one would ever believe it was the wealthy and well-educated Leopold and Loeb who committed the crime.

Pre-meditated Murder of the Highest Degree

For seven long months, throughout the winter and into the spring Leopold and Loeb spent hours planning the details of their dangerous game. Though money was inconsequential to the duo, who hailed from millionaires, nevertheless, they agreed on a ten-thousand-dollar ransom.

Their plan consisted of scouting the perfect victim, writing and delivering a ransom note, and then having the child's parents deliver the funds. To get their hands on the cash without being identified they decided that they would demand their victim's father toss an envelope containing the money from the southbound train out of Chicago along the elevated tracks west of Lake Michigan. Waiting in a car below they would be able to grab the money and flee.

They brainstormed their ideal victim and quickly put in motion an elaborate scheme to cover their tracks. Unfortunately, when it came to murder Leopold and Loeb were not the perfect criminals, instead, they were dimwitted sadists.

To begin, they created false identities for each other, and one full month before the murder, they used these identities to secure the tools needed for kidnapping and killing.

On April 20, Leopold presented himself as Morton D. Ballard at a Chicago car rental dealership. He said he was a traveling salesman and needed a car. He claimed that the only identification he had on himself at the time was a banknote. You see, earlier that morning the two had visited a bank and set up an account for the fake Mr. Ballard. They had also checked him into The Morrison, a local hotel.

To make these personas infallible, Leopold and Loeb went to incredible lengths. They typed out fake letters to Mr. Ballard and had them delivered to the hotel. When Leopold was told renting a car required references, he stationed Loeb at a drugstore payphone. When the dealership checked the references, Loeb was ready and waiting to provide an upstanding review under the name Mr. Louis Mason.

With the hotel, bank account, and car secured the teens drove around for a few hours and then returned the vehicle. Unfortunately, upon returning to the hotel they found their belongings, a briefcase with old magazines, missing. A maid thought it odd that no one was actually staying in the room and had reported the case. While it wasn't incriminating, the two never returned to the hotel for fear of suspicion and attention.

On May 20, they pulled up to a hardware store in Leopold's cherry red sports car. The pair purchased what would become the murder weapons: rope, a chisel, and tape. They then went to buy hydrochloric acid from a drugstore. At Leopold's home, they taped the chisel to form a club, created a gag with fabric, and typed a ransom note.

The note was produced on the typewriter that had been stolen from Leopold's fraternity. A typewriter that had a few easily identifiable damaged keys. In summary, the note read: *Don't communicate with police, gather $10,000 in old bills, be home by 1 o'clock to receive a call with further instructions.* The note left a blank spot to be filled in later with the details specific to their chosen victim.

The next chilling step was to choose the child, someone young and wealthy. The financial status was key as no one would suspect the two trust-fund boys to be the killers. It also indicated that the murder was solely an ego trip, there was no real motive other than to watch the police struggle to figure out the crime while the public hung on every clue and detail.

On May 21, the false Mr. Ballard rented a car again and they ditched Leo's sports car behind the back of his house. They pulled into town and parked outside the Harvard Boys school where they had both previously attended. As they waited for classes to end for the day, Leopold hid in an alley. Loeb scouted the school grounds, eventually meeting a teacher and young child, chatting with both of them.

It is clear by this point that the two had no idea what they were doing, having returned to a school where people knew them and talking to many individuals who could later be used as witnesses. Loeb even bumped into his own brother, who went to the school. Nevertheless, there were several groups of kids and they settled on one named John Levinson.

After returning to Leopold's house to grab bird-watching binoculars, and checking a drugstore phonebook for the boy's address they drove back to the spot where they had last sighted Levinson. He had run off. While the bumbling murderers were disappointed, they were not deterred.

As their car crawled along, they stumbled upon Loeb's second cousin, fourteen-year-old Bobby Franks. They knew that his family was very well off and they were aware of Bobby's love of sports. When Bobby initially declined their offered ride, Loeb persuaded him into the car by tempting him with a conversation about a new tennis racket.

As soon as Bobby was in the front passenger seat Leopold drove off and Loeb attacked. With one hand muffling the boy's mouth he bludgeoned his skull with the makeshift club. Bobby struggled to fight off his attackers as Loeb struck him repeatedly. Bobby continued to wail, Leopold and Loeb were wholly unprepared for how difficult it is to end a life, so they decided to gag him with the rag and tape his mouth shut.

Bobby Franks suffocated to death in the backseat of the car. They wrapped his body in a blanket and drove nearly fifteen miles to Indiana. When they approached the border, they tossed Bobby's shoes into a bush and removed his socks and trousers. Then they stopped for dinner at a diner and none of the clients inside had any clue that an adolescent's body lay in the vehicle in the parking lot. When it was dark, they traveled to their predetermined dumping site.

Though they had intended to murder their victim with an ether-soaked rag at the site, Bobby was already dead. There was nothing left to do but remove all his clothes and pour acid on his face and body in an attempt to disguise his identity.

The cold-blooded killers then tried to shove his body into a railway car but it wouldn't budge more than halfway. Leopold struggled with the exposed corpse but ultimately left Bobby's lower half visible. They left the crime scene and unknowingly left behind Leopold's horn-rimmed glasses that had fallen from his pocket as he wrestled with the body.

They enacted the rest of their plan. Delivering the ransom note typed on the faulty typewriter, phoning Bobby's parents with their demand, and waiting for the excitement to really begin.

Chicago was no stranger to bloodbaths at the time, with the likes of Al Capone terrorizing the streets. However, the murder of a wealthy child from the suburbs was something entirely different.

Confession of a Senseless Crime

The killers' craving for noir-style drama didn't play out as planned. They struggled to clean the blood from the rental car, even being caught by the chauffeur and making an excuse that they had spilled wine. Bobby's father forgot the address provided by Loeb, where he was supposed to receive further instruction. Then, the dumb duo was dealt the final blow.

They passed a newsstand whose front page read: "Boy's body found in swamp." In less than twenty-four hours, the body of Bobby Frank had already been found and was quickly identified. With no need to complete the ransom, the anxiety-riddled geniuses returned home and worked to cover their tracks, tossing the typewriter in the river and burning the blanket.

However, one piece of evidence remained. A very particular pair of horn-rimmed glasses discovered at the crime scene emblazoned with the optometrist's name.

Said doctor had only ever sold three pairs of the distinctive glasses. Two of the individuals were quickly dismissed, only Leopold remained.

When questioned, he made up a lackluster excuse that he had been out there the week prior on a bird-watching excursion and must have dropped his glasses. But when the destroyed typewriter was discovered on June 7, the two were brought in for questioning.

Loeb was the first to confess, blaming Leopold for the actual murder. Upon learning of his incrimination, Leopold quickly confessed his version, placing the crime on Loeb. Still, most of their stories corroborated the evidence police had turned up and rendered them guilty.

Leopold and Loeb were shameless. They seemed to feel no remorse and cited their motives as intellectual; wanting to commit the perfect murder and fulfill their Nietzche delusions. Leopold in particular was very forthcoming, stating, "I was interested in learning what it would feel like to be a murderer, and I am sorry to report that I feel the same as ever."

The media had a field day with the case. While they may have not committed the crime of the century, they certainly attained the trial of the century. Loeb's family hired the infamous Clarence Darrow to try and keep their son from capital punishment.

After much deliberation, the judge withheld execution due to Loeb and Leopold's young age. He sentenced each of them to ninety-nine years in prison for the kidnapping and life in prison for the murder. The once bright and promising futures of the boys were rapidly extinguished thanks to their ridiculous notions that they were above the law of man and of the powers that be.

Loeb died at thirty years old in 1936, after he was stabbed in the showers by a fellow prison inmate.

Leopold was granted parole in 1958, after serving thirty-three years. He no longer had visions of grandeur, stating, "All I want... is to become a humble little person."

The cold-blooded killer lived out his days in obscurity in Puerto Rico. Eventually marrying, studying at university, and even returning to Chicago on occasion to visit old friends.

He died of a heart attack, a much nicer fate than the one Bobby Frank's met on that fateful day in May.

The murder of an innocent child purely for the sake of thrill-seeking and as a test of knowledge will forever be a part of Chicago's blood-soaked history.

VIII
Hinterkaifeck Murders

ACROSS THE POND, GERMANY IN THE 1920S WAS the opposite of the American glitz and glam. The country was devastated by war and slowly trying to regain its foothold as they began to modernize. Outside of the cities, many Germans lived as they always had. Quiet lives, tending to crops, caring for farm animals, and enjoying the pleasantries of small-town life.

One such village was Kaifeck. Only, the calm rural peace of this village would be irreparably shattered in April of 1922. A nearby family, who lived and worked the Hinterkaifeck farmstead would be savagely murdered in a manner so appalling, that it still shocks people to this day. As recently as 1986, suspects have been interviewed in an attempt to solve the cold case. However, out of the one hundred or so people questioned, no one has been identified as the maniacal Hinterkaifeck murderer.

Footsteps, Bad Feelings, and Fear

The Hinterkaifeck farmstead was situated half a mile behind the town of Kaifeck and about an hour's drive from Munich. It was a sprawling farm that contained a variety of animals and crops, all cared for by the Gabriel family and their relatives, the Grubers. The children attended the nearby school and the adults ventured into town now and again to retrieve mail and supplies.

But the Hinterkaifeck farmstead was a lonesome place, flanked by woods and bringing in very few visitors. The family could go for days or even weeks at a time without seeing outsiders, especially when school was out of session. While this may lead you to believe they led a quiet and tranquil life, the isolation of the farm could be eerie at times.

Thirty-five-year-old Viktoria Gabriel, a widow, owned the farm. She had two children, seven-year-old Cäzilia and two-year-old Josef. Viktoria's aging parents, Andreas and Cäzilia Gruber, also resided on the homestead. To help care for the children amidst the never-ending farm chores, the Gabriel family also employed a maid.

Six months or so before the murders, the longtime maid suddenly quit. On too many occasions she stated she had a run-in with what she referred to as the supernatural.

When the children were outside playing and all the adults working on the property, the maid would hear voices. They couldn't be explained and had no known source. Especially disconcerting were the voices heard at night in the darkness, unidentifiable but definitely threatening. The former maid would later tell police that she always had the feeling of being watched, and that strange noises could be heard coming from the unoccupied attic.

Around November 1921, the maid declared the house haunted, and tendered her resignation.

She wasn't the only one to experience strange happenings on the farm during this period. Once Andreas found a newspaper in his home, which in and of itself wasn't odd except for the fact that it didn't belong to him or any of the other family members. No one had been out to purchase the newspaper and they could not figure out how it came to rest in their residence.

Then, he reported to his neighbors that one morning after a snowfall he found a set of footprints. The tracks were pristine, and the snow had not been disturbed, Andreas was the first one out that morning. Suspiciously, the trail of prints led from the forest to the farmhouse. As he walked about the property, he could not locate a set of prints traveling away from the home. They led directly from the forest to his door and then disappeared.

Finally, a few days before the murder, the Hinterkaifeck members reported one of the keys to their home missing. They only had two, so the loss of one was glaringly obvious. It was never recovered. These occurrences were never reported to the police, only noted in small-town chatter between neighbors. If only they had been supernatural in nature, the Gruber family may have not met such a horrifying and bloody end.

A Disturbing Discovery

On April 1, 1922, the residents of the Hinterkaifeck farm were conspicuously missing. Though the family was known for keeping to themselves, their absence was beginning to be noticed. Seven-year-old Cäzilia had not shown up for school two days in a row. Viktoria missed choir practice at the church, and the entire family did not arrive for the sermon. The mailman also noticed that the family's letters were beginning to pile up at the post office. By April 4, neighbors decided they should organize a trip out to the farm. Lorenz Schlittenbauer led the search party. They likely thought they were going to find them bedridden with an illness or befallen by some minor tragedy that prohibited them from journeying into town. They were wholly unprepared for what horrors awaited them.

From afar, everything seemed normal. The animals were in the pasture, their feed barrels stocked and their water troughs full. But the farm was unsettlingly quiet.

In the barn, the group of neighbors discovered the first bloodbath. Four bodies lay buried under the hay. Each one covered in gruesome marks. In the home were two more bodies, each with devastating wounds.

The entire household had been slaughtered; but when and by who? It was a sight the visitors wouldn't soon forget, and they wanted answers. Soon after the bodies were discovered, autopsies were performed.

The results of the inquiries into the deaths of the Hinterkaifeck residents are perhaps even more stomach-churning than the initial discovery. One by one four family members had somehow been lured away from the house and into the barn. Once in the barn, they met a grisly fate.

Cäzilia, the grandmother was strangled. She was then struck on the head seven times, fracturing her skull. Her husband Andreas was found with the skin of his face shredded, his cheekbones peeking through. Viktoria's skull was also fractured and lent some hint as to the murder weapon. There were nine wounds in total, each one was "star-shaped" and the side of her face indicated that she was beaten with a blunt object.

Unfortunately, Cäzilia the elder, Andreas, and Viktoria fared far better than young Cäzilia. They all died instantly while the seven-year-old likely lay in shock for hours. The bones of her lower jaw were splintered, her face and neck were pockmarked with circular, gaping wounds. Chunks of her hair had been torn from her scalp, not by the murderer but likely by her own hands as a result of the shock and pain.

In the house lay the new maid, Maria Baumgartner, killed in her dressing room on her very first day of work. She was assaulted with crosswise blows to the head and quickly died. Josef, the baby, suffered a direct and severe blow to his face while lying in his cot. While the bodies in the barn were covered with hay, in the house

Maria's body was draped in sheets and Josef was covered in one of his mother's dresses.

It was thought that the weapon used was a mattock, a tool used for digging that resembles a pickaxe. While the violence of the murders is extremely distressing, the story only gets more chilling.

The family pets and animals, a Pomeranian watchdog, and a herd of livestock were all unharmed. In fact, they were in perfect health having been cared for in the week between the murders and the discovery. Neighbors even recalled seeing smoke coming from the chimney of the Gruber home in the days following the deaths. The killer had cared for the farm, lived in the house, ate meals, and prepared fires in the hearth. All the while, the house's original occupants lay slaughtered upstairs and in the barn a few yards away.

Police searched in vain for the murderer. Initially suspecting vagrants or men of ill repute. But nothing in the house had been disturbed or taken, the large sums of cash belonging to the Gruebers lay untouched.

Investigators then turned to men who were known to visit the farm or had a relationship with the family. Viktoria's husband was a casualty of war, and the father of her young son Josef forever remained a mystery. The leader of the search party, Lorenz Schlittenbauer, was long suspected to be the child's true father and at one time the couple had proclaimed it so.

But Viktoria's father had denied the rumors and put an end to the pair's romance. Lorenz eventually remarried and started a family, but their baby died shortly after birth. Police guessed that he was devastated by the loss of his child and unwilling to pay child support for Josef unless the two were married, so he went to the farm and killed them all. This suspicion was strengthened by the fact that other search party members reported that Lorenz was unphased by the bodies and handled them without repulsion.

Even though he was questioned repeatedly, police were never able to pin the murders on him, citing shock as the cause of his odd behavior. They then turned to Viktoria's first husband, Karl, surmising that he returned from the war and murdered his family. But they soon found out that he had been slain in France and several soldiers attested to seeing his body.

Finally, the police pointed the finger at a member of the Gruber/Gabriel family. In the next town over, his "proclivities for incest and abuse" were well-known. Could Josef be the offspring of Viktoriya and her own father? It was believed that he had many children with women other than Cäzilia, though most of them had not survived childhood as a result of their father's violence. They surmised that one of the farm's residents could have killed their relatives before turning the mattock on themselves. Only none of the wounds appeared to be self-inflicted, ruling out that theory.

The only facts the police knew to be true were that the murderer knew their way around the farm as evidenced by the care of the animals, the state of the home, and how expertly they wielded the mattock. The severity of the murders led police to believe the killer had a vendetta against some member of the family.

Authorities also thought that the killer had actually been living in the home undetected for some time. Silently watching the family, waiting for the perfect moment. It would explain the footprints leading to the home, the strange sounds from the attic, the suspicious newspaper, and the missing key.

With no additional suspects and no further murders, police eventually closed the case.

Secrets of the Skulls

Shortly after the autopsies were finished, the bodies were beheaded and sent to Munich to be examined by Clairvoyants for metaphysical clues. The skulls remained silent, not giving up any secrets.

In WWII, the skulls were lost. The family was buried, headless, in a plot in Waidhofen.

Their farm was demolished in 1923.

Over the past ninety-eight years, the case has been reopened numerous times.

The murderer, where of this world or supernatural in nature, was never found.

IX

Turtle Lake Murders

NORTH DAKOTA IN THE 1920S WAS FAR FROM the hubbub of America's more notorious cities. It didn't have the Broadway Butterflies or the bootleggers and mob men of the metropolises. Unfortunately, this doesn't mean that this rural state was spared crime and bloodshed.

The spring of 1920 was when one of North Dakota's worst mass murders took place. All of those killed belonged to the same family. Only one family member escaped; an infant, the youngest member of the family who was barely a year. She lived until 2003, not moving far from the farm where her relatives were brutally murdered.

What really took place on that fateful day in April 1920 may never be known. The last words of the convicted murderer hinted that he took the blame for the real killers and would die protecting them. Here is the story of the Wolf Family of Turtle Lake.

From Well-To-Do, to Dead

The Wolf family farm was very prosperous in the late 1910s and early 1920s. The head of the household, Jacob Wolf, was well-known throughout the Turtle Lake community. Neighbors admired him for his farming practices that always left his land tidy and his animals well cared for.

He was also a wonderful father to his six daughters, aged eight months to thirteen years old, and husband to his wife Beata. Despite him being an upstanding member of the community, neighbors recall Jacob Wolf mentioning a vengeful enemy.

He'd previously had a dispute with one of his close neighbors, though no one thought the disagreement would ever come to blows. It wasn't in either man's nature. Nevertheless, one friend remembers Jacob Wolf fearing for his life, stopping him as he passed by and confiding that a "neighbor may harm him."

Unfortunately, Jacob's friend thought it was just a silly suspicion and didn't report the odd encounter until it was too late.

In April of 1920, the North Dakota spring was chilly and wet. When the sun made a rare appearance, housewives dashed to hang their laundry on the clothesline to dry before the next rain shower. It struck neighbors passing by the Wolf farm as odd that Ms. Wolf would leave her laundry on the line for an entire day and night. Getting blown by the gusty wind and dampened by the drizzle.

John Kraft was on his way into Turtle Lake when his suspicion got the better of him, noticing the same clothes and sheets flapping in the breeze that he had passed a few days earlier. A neighbor to the Wolf Farm, he decided to check in on the family.

By now you should know that neighbors with the best intentions often stumble upon the most brutal and grizzly of scenes.

John stopped his vehicle and set off through the yard toward the house. However, before he could reach the porch something else struck him as odd. The door of a nearby barn was left ajar and banged against the wall with each gust of wind. From inside the barn, he could hear frenzied pigs rooting.

When Kraft entered the barn there amongst the pigs and the hay were three partially exposed bodies. Carelessly covered with hay and debris lay the corpses of Jacob Wolf and Maria and Edna, two of his daughters.

As John made his way into the home to look for the others, he stumbled upon more horrors. Five more bodies lay in the cellar of the house. They belonged to Beata Wolf, three more of the couple's daughters, and a thirteen-year-old hired farmhand related to the family through marriage.

The family had not been completely extinguished though. In a bedroom, still in her cradle, lay eight-month-old Emma. She was dressed in a light gown and was listless from cold and hunger, but alive. The sole survivor of the Wolf Family.

Baiting a Killer

John Kraft hastily telephoned the sheriff. Sheriff Stefferud arrived at Turtle Lake that evening and decided to spend the night in the Wolf's home along with three of the farm's neighbors. The family was obviously murdered, most of the bodies possessing bullet holes and a few of them bashed skulls. The sheriff believed that murderers often return to the scene of the crime, and if he waited long enough perhaps the sadistic killer would show up.

Unfortunately, as the investigation was ongoing, the eight mangled bodies could not be removed from the property, so the men sat in the darkness, surrounded by the decaying corpses, watching and waiting.

Around five thirty the next morning, Sheriff Stefferud's patience paid off. The other men had just driven off to grab breakfast when Stefferud stepped outside. In the dim light, he could see another car approaching the farm.

A man pulled up to the house, and got out of the car, unaware he was being watched from the shadows. He then walked up to the house and peered through the living room window before purposely setting off toward the barn. The man froze when Stefferud announced his presence; with his hands raised he identified himself as Henry Layer.

Henry's farm was about a mile and a half down the road from the Wolf's homestead and the men waiting with the sheriff would have had to pass it on their way into town. As Stefferud talked with Henry he suspected that he had seen the car go by and thought the farm was unoccupied, not realizing the sheriff had stayed behind.

The sheriff also had another suspicion. Henry never removed his right hand from the pocket of his pants. This behavior was odd when they were chatting but became even more strange when Henry inserted himself on that morning's investigation of the farm. As Henry made trivial observations and suggested silly procedures, Stefferud observed that his hand steadfastly remained in his pocket.

Things came to a head when Henry curiously suggested they check the barn where the family was slain for eggs. One man, Bossert, went with him. Henry picked through the hay before pointing out a clutch of eggs. As Bossert bent to retrieve them, Henry yelled, "Look what I've found." He opened his hand, showing the empty shotgun shells.

When Henry triumphantly returned with his evidence, the sheriff keenly noted that his hand was no longer in his pocket, and he claimed to have found the shells in an area of hay that had been thoroughly turned over by investigators.

By that afternoon, hundreds of people were at the Wolf's place. Some gawkers, some police, and some of the most well-known investigators in the state. Only one more clue was found on the farm, the murder weapon. A double-barrel shotgun whose stock was found sticking out of a slough near the Wolf residence.

Over the next couple of days, two men were arrested and released, a youth was questioned and then freed, and rewards were posted in the tribune. Farms all over the rural community lived in a state of panic. Fathers staying up all night with their rifles cocked, waiting for a maniac killer to come for their family.

Sheriff Stefferud never got over the weird incident with Henry Layer. Then, a neighbor confirmed his suspicions. Henry Layer and Jacob Wolf had quarreled. Henry's cows had wandered onto Jacob's farm and one of them had even suffered injuries from the Wolf family dog.

On the following Wednesday, a funeral service was held at the Wolf farm. It was attended by a humongous crowd, among the mourners was Henry Layer, who was declaring what a horrible shame it was, but at the same time eerily suggesting the lids of the eight coffins be removed so he could gaze upon the faces of his neighbors one last time.

While the last rites were being given, investigators were at the Layer farm. They questioned one of his daughters who admitted her father had been absent for much of the week the murders took place.

Confessing to the Crime

It took the police nearly a month to gather enough circumstantial evidence to arrest Henry. They took him in for questioning, but he maintained his innocence. Until finally, he confessed.

Henry detailed how ill feelings had long been brewing between him and Jacob Wolf. Things boiled over when he walked through the Wolf farm and into their house, demanding payment for the injury of his cow by Wolf's dog.

Jacob refused to pay and demanded that Henry leave the property. When he refused Jacob grabbed his double-barrel shotgun. They struggled over the weapon. Henry claims during the fight the gun was discharged twice, one bullet striking Jacob's wife and the other their young farmhand. Both fell dead onto the kitchen floor.

Jacob fled the house, running for the yard, but Henry quickly reloaded and struck him in the back. Two of the Wolf daughters, having just seen their parents and a child murdered, took off screaming toward the barn.

Henry pursued them. He fired, hitting one girl cleanly in the head. As the other child cowered and begged for mercy Henry brought the barrel up to her skull and pulled the trigger. He then fired another bullet into the first girl and returned to the house.

The remaining three daughters were yelling and crying and he fired the shotgun at two of them, killing them instantly. The third he assaulted with a hatchet, bashing in her skull.

He then dragged Jacob's body into the barn beside the two dead girls and covered them with straw. He went back to the house, rounded up the five slain victims, and deposited their bodies in the cellar.

He broke the shotgun deliberately to conceal the murder weapon and buried it in a slough. He weaved his way back home, taking a meandering path, and then meticulously cleaned the blood from his body and clothing. He did not tell his wife or his family where he had been.

Henry claimed that "The reason I did not kill the baby was, I believe, because I did not go into the room in which the baby lay."

He said that he didn't intend to commit murder, but after the gun accidentally discharged his mind cracked and events became hazy.

He pleaded guilty in front of a judge and was sentenced to life in prison. Sometime later, Layer would die following an operation for appendicitis.

The murder was one of North Dakota's most violent. The events remained fresh in people's minds for a long time. What would cause a man to snap like that? Ruthlessly murdering little girls when he had daughters of the same age at home?

Years later, investigators reviewing the case found that the police did not have strong evidence against Henry Layer.

In fact, in jail, Henry wrote an affidavit proclaiming his innocence. He stated the grilling and coercion by police was intense. "(He) told me that if I would not say what he wanted he would beat my brains out. I then gave up, started to cry, and said that I would do and say what they wanted." Henry detailed how the police beat him, made him stand until he passed out, and convinced him there was a mob outside waiting to hang him.

Law enforcement denied these claims. But a prison doctor and barber would later attest to the fact that they believed Henry had been beaten. Investigators looking at the case with fresh eyes also noted that parts of Henry's story didn't match up with details of the case, like the positioning of the bodies or the timing of events.

If Henry didn't savagely murder Jacob and Beata Wolf, and their innocent children, then who did? Experts believe that Henry either had accomplices or witnessed the murder and decided not to disclose who the true killers were. He took the fall while diabolic killers who could crush a little girl's skull with a hatchet roamed free in Turtle Lake.

X
William Edward Hickman

THE MURDER OF MARION PARKER IS SUNG about in folk ballads. Lyrics tell the story of a young girl deceived, kidnapped, and then extinguished. But the true tale is much more horrific than the guitar-laden songs make it out to be.

A heartless and sadistic killer who idolized murderous monsters and desired to follow in their footsteps. This is the story of William Edward Hickman and poor, little Marion Parker.

Dangerous Deception

California during the 1920s was rich with crime. Bizarre stories of kidnapping, assault, and murder graced the headlines nearly every day. Los Angeles and other thriving cities were no stranger to the frenzied and blood-soaked craziness of the era.

By 1935, LA was known as the "City of Headline Murders," a title it had been earning since the early twenties. In 1927, crime was at its peak.

William Edward Hickman was nineteen at the time. He lived near Pasadena and worked at a bank in downtown Los Angeles. He loved poring over the details of the latest gruesome murder. Like someone eagerly awaiting the Sunday crossword, William looked forward to the obituaries and obscene recounting of deaths.

His favorite clippings were the accounts of Leopold and Loeb, a pair of intellectually extraordinary young men who decided to murder a young child "for the thrill of it." William had his mind set on committing a similar crime. Like his idols, he was both mentally unstable and sadistic enough to follow through with it.

On December 15, 1927, just over a week before Christmas, William put his plan into action. He showed up at an LA school. Well dressed and very articulate, he had no problem deceiving the academic staff. William told school officials that the father of two of their students, twins Marion and Marjorie Parker, had become seriously ill. The girls' father, Perry Parker, had requested that the younger daughter, Marion, come at once to be by his side.

Though the teacher was a bit confused by the request, William quickly interjected that he meant the "smaller of the two girls" and that time was of the essence. He said that the teacher could contact Perry Parker's associates at the bank where he worked to confirm the story, but his seemingly good-faith suggestion allayed her fears and she sent Marion off with William.

It was only hours later when Marion did not return home from school with her twin, did people realize that she had been kidnapped. By this point, the twelve-year-old had been in William's custody for many hours and he had confessed to her that she was being kidnapped and held for ransom.

William Hickman was a touch delusional. Though he wasn't certifiably insane, he had ideas of grandeur that did not fit reality. He also had been a fervently religious youth, but at some point, it had crossed over into perverse mysticism and narcissism. This was evidenced by his odd confessions describing the kidnap and murder.

William claimed that when he told Marion of his plans, she treated it as a thrilling adventure. "We were driving out in Hollywood Friday night, when my car was stopped by a traffic light," stated William in a jailhouse interview. "Marion was beside me and the newsboys waved their papers close by us. Marion seemed to be amused by this."

Whether or not this is true, the young girl's excitement probably turned to fear rather quickly.

Ransom and Religion

Marion's parents, the Parkers, quickly called the police to report her disappearance and abduction by a strange man at her school. Not long after, they received two telegrams sent by a "George Fox" — one hailing from Pasadena and the other from Alhambra. They warned the family not to interfere with the kidnapper's plans, which was extortion, as the telegrams also cautioned the family to be on the lookout for further ransom instructions.

The next day a ransom note appeared, emblazoned with the symbols Δ ε α τ η, or "death" written with Greek characters. It read: "Fox is my name, very sly you know. Get this straight. Your daughter's life hangs by a thread and I have a Gillette ready and able to handle the situation."

The second note followed shortly after, again with the header Δ ε α τ η. The sender signed "Fox-fate," instructed Marion's parents to get fifteen hundred dollars in twenty dollar gold certificates and be ready to complete a drop that evening. Perhaps most chilling was the addition of a note written by Marion herself, begging her father to comply in fear of what William had threatened to do. It read: "Please, Daddy, I want to come home tonight. Your loving daughter, Marion Parker."

Parker quickly gathered the money, close to twenty thousand dollars' worth today, and readied himself to meet the kidnapper. William called Parker on December 16 and outlined the plan; but when it came time, he spotted police in the area and the hand-off never occurred.

William was enraged. He sent another note blaming Parker for the failed exchange. The ramblings of his notes became increasingly delusional and diabolical, stating, "I will be two billion times as cautious and clever, as deadly from now on. You have brought this on yourself, and you deserve it and worse. A man who betrays his love for his own daughter is a second Judas Iscariot — many times more wicked than the worst modern criminal. If you want aid against me, ask God, not man..." He also included another note from Marion.

Around seven thirty on December 17, Mr. Parker was waiting for the kidnapper on the corner of 5th Avenue and South Manhattan Street in Los Angeles. William exited a nearby vehicle and approached the apprehensive father.

His hand holding a gun aimed at Mr. Parker, William said, "You know what I am here for. No monkey business."

"Can I see my little girl?" asked Mr. Parker.

William motioned toward his car. Mr. Parker could just make out Marion's form. She lay motionless on the seat, her body in some sort of tightly tied package. Mr. Parker assumed she had been chloroformed to make the exchange easier.

He handed over seventy-five twenty dollar gold certificates. William got in his car and drove about a block away, then shoved the girl out onto the street.

Mr. Parker ran to his daughter, sweeping her up in his arms, then let out a soul-searing cry of grief.

Marion was not chloroformed, but dead. The package around her neck was loosened to reveal a disturbing scene. All that lay beneath the covering was her torso. Her arms and legs had been severed at the joints. Just above her brow, a wire had been wrapped so tightly that it bit into her skin and her flesh gaped open. The scene only became grislier.

The twelve-year-old had been disemboweled and rags took up the space where her entrails once were. She had also been viciously beaten and flogged.

The coroner revealed that she had been killed around twelve hours before and died either from asphyxiation or blood loss. The next day, December 18, Marion's arms and legs were recovered, found in a park wrapped in packages similar to the one that contained her head and torso.

Capture and Confessions

The police were now searching in earnest for the man who could commit such vicious atrocities against a twelve-year-old child. The reward for the capture of the criminal topped fifty thousand dollars.

Spurred on by not only the reward but sheer disgust at the murderer's actions, hundreds of police and thousands of angry citizens began looking for Marion's killer. It would turn out to be the largest manhunt in the history of the West Coast.

Mr. Parker identified the object of their efforts as "a young white man, around twenty-five, about five foot eight, weighing one hundred fifty pounds. Smooth shaven, dark wavy hair, and thin features. He had pushed Marion's body out of a Ford Roadster and driven away."

One of the shirts Marion's disfigured body was wrapped in contained a clue, a laundry mark that police traced to an apartment house. Over one hundred cops performed a room-by-room search of the building. They turned up one renter, a "Donald Evans," who matched the perpetrator's description, but a search of his room yielded no clues.

However, they did locate the Ford Roadster, reported stolen out of Kansas City just a week prior. And, as luck would have it the vehicle was not wiped down of fingerprints. Police found their match, a petty thief and forger by the name of William Edward Hickman.

Mr. Parker remembered Hickman, a former employee of the bank who worked as an assistant cashier. During his time at the bank, Hickman had a poor track record. Often late for work and impartial to authority, his financial career ended when he was accused of stealing from the bank via attempted forgery. As one of his supervisors, Parker had testified at William's forgery trial. He opposed the sentencing recommendation of probation and lobbied for a harsher punishment. William served time as a result.

The landlady of the apartment building police had searched came forward. William's mugshot was all over the newspapers, and she could confirm that "Donald Evans" and William Hickman were one and the same. A secondary search of the apartment turned up human blood.

Eight thousand local, state, and federal officers listed William Hickman as their top priority. But he continued to elude police, somehow making it past an intense police checkpoint; stealing cars, and passing gold certificates in Seattle, then Portland, Oregon.

Finally, on December 22, William Hickman was apprehended. He confessed and was extradited to California.

William's complete confession was long and twisted. He claimed he'd had an accomplice who killed Marion after he had kidnapped her from school, only the person he named was in jail at the time of the crime. He then stated that he only kidnapped her for ransom so he could pay for college.

His description of the actual murder flip-flopped between illogical and disturbing. At one point he said that Marion was thrilled with the entire thing, and went along with his plan, telling him that, "In daydreams at her desk in school she had also imagined this, being kidnapped." Later he detailed how he strangled Marion before slitting her throat but believed she was still alive as he began to dismember her.

His reasoning he claimed was that a "Divine Providence" appeared to him and told him to murder Marion, as it was a test set before him to see if he was "super strong and capable of the work."

Police were baffled by William. He was once a bright pupil, popular with his class, and a high achiever academically. He had left high school with a plan to study ministry, not to become a sadistic killer.

William retained the boastful and haughty attitude he possessed as praised intellectual and spoke nonchalantly about the murder as if he was recounting a passage from a textbook. Once in prison, he attempted to lay the groundwork for an insanity plea, probing the prison guards about how an insane person would act and speak.

Experts examined him during his trial, some finding him sane while others declared him mentally unstable. Prison staff, witnesses, and others testified to his sanity while his own mother declared that "insanity ran in the family" when it was her turn on the stand.

William remained unphased, spouting off comments like, "Do you think I will get as much notoriety as Leopold and Loeb?" and "He won't hang me. He doesn't believe in capital punishment," referencing the judge.

After ten days, the jury found him both sane and guilty. He was sentenced to death by hanging.

With a smile, William told reporters, "The state won by a neck."

On October 19, 1928, William Edward Hickman went to the gallows. He never expressed remorse or sorrow for his actions. His final words were, "Warden, tell me they're going to bury me here. Honest I don't want my old man and my mother to spend a lot of money taking me back east."

Was he insane? Did he really do it all for cash? Or, were his reasons more sinister, such as to get revenge against Mr. Parker for sending him to jail? Or to gain as much publicity as Leopold and Loeb for a similarly disturbing crime?

We will forever grapple with the same questions the jury did in 1928, before condemning a man to death.

XI

Louise Peete

LOUISE PEETE WAS ONE OF AMERICA'S FIRST black widows. She loved to boast about the lovers she drove to death nearly as much as she bragged about her sexual escapades. Fallen from grace, the once polished lady took to burying boyfriends and friends after she no longer had use for them.

From Massachusetts to Texas, Louise left a trail of bodies in her wake.

A Southern Belle

Lofie Louise Preslar was born to a wealthy publisher father and a high society mother.. Her privileged upbringing afforded her the best schools, high-class social gatherings, and all the trappings of a lavish life. However, there was one thing teenage Louise was denied, and that was romantic affairs.

Louise began to gain a reputation for her sexual escapades and eventually, her notoriety got her kicked out of one of Louisiana's most posh finishing schools. The expelled debutante moved back home to Bienville and looked for other ways to pass the time.

In 1903, she met and married Henry Bosley, a traveling salesman. Louise decided to join him on the road. Their marriage and Henry's life were both cut short when he came home one day to find Louise in bed with a local oilman. Overtaken with grief over the fact that Louise would cheat on him, he killed himself.

Henry was victim number one in what would become a long line of lovers who would end up dead after entering into a relationship with Louise. Louise was unphased by this turn of events. She promptly sold all his belongings and moved to Shreveport.

Back in Louisiana, she took up her old trade, except this time for money. She became a prostitute and a favorite among the local gentry. Louise often made house calls to her clients while their wives were away. This worked out wonderfully as it also afforded her the opportunity to pocket some of their jewelry, unbeknownst to their cheating husbands.

Louise became more and more greedy, both with her relationships and her stealing. Eventually, she was discovered. To avoid exposure and ultimately jail, she moved to Waco, Texas.

Texas was flush with black gold because of the recently discovered oil reserves scattered across the state ,Louise just needed to get her hands on a man who benefited from Texas's booming oil industry. She set her sights on a wealthy and wiley oilman named Joe Appel. He was known for his unapologetically lavish lifestyle. He was covered in diamonds from head to toe. They studded his shirt buttons, belt buckle, and encrusted his numerous rings. Joe was the perfect man for Louise.

To Murder, not to Marry

Just one week after their meeting, wildcat Joe was found dead. He had been shot in the head. Louise testified in front of a grand jury that she had shot him, but maintained it was in self-defense as he had tried to rape her.

But the Texas jury wasn't familiar with Louise, and they also glossed over the fact that Joe's diamonds were mysteriously missing. By the time Louise finished spinning her tale of fighting off the egotistical Joe and protecting her virtue, the jury was applauding and found her undeniably not guilty.

The profit Louise made from Joe's jewels didn't last her long and soon she was back on the market for another man to murder... I mean to marry.

Harry Faurote, a local hotel clerk, fit the bill just fine. He had a steady income and Louise knew she could find her thrills elsewhere. Only Harry couldn't take her repeated adultery and ended up hanging himself in the hotel's basement.

It was time for Louise to move on before anyone could get suspicious. She traveled to Denver, where she met Richard Peete, another door-to-door salesman. While something must have gone right in the relationship for Louise to keep Richard around long enough to bear him a daughter, she soon became bored. Not long after the birth, she abandoned her family for the glittering streets of Los Angeles.

LA in the 1920s was flush with wealth and crime. Louise coveted both. While looking for a place to live she met mining executive Jacob Denton. The unsuspecting Denton was instantly charmed. Though he had a house to rent he quickly decided to hold onto the property for him and his new lover. Louise thought she could seal the deal, and after a few weeks of intense passion she proposed. Denton refused.

Louise took the refusal quite well, or so it seemed. She decided that as a treat for Denton she would raise mushrooms in the home's basement, after all, they were his favorite delicacy. The way to a man's heart is through his stomach, right? Louise asked the caretaker to dump a ton of soil in the basement.

Unfortunately, the only fungi Denton would get his hands on would be the decay forming on his corpse. He disappeared on May 30, 1920. Suspicious callers began to wonder what happened to the mining tycoon. Louise was prepared.

He fought with a Spanish-looking woman who chopped off his arm, she stated. He survived but was embarrassed by his disfigurement and had gone into seclusion. When Denton's lawyer pressed to see his client Louise further embellished the story, adding an amputated leg. Shockingly her tales of shame and learning how to use artificial limbs before appearing in public held off suspicion for months. In the meantime, Louise continued to live a life of luxury, throwing lavish parties in the home.

Nearly six months after his disappearance, Denton's lawyer's curiosity got the better of him. He demanded that police search the property. A few shovels of soil in the basement revealed Jacob Denton with a bullet in his skull. Louise was long gone by this time, having fled to Denver, and resumed family life with Richard Peete and their daughter.

The police tracked her down and put her on trial. In January 1921, she was sentenced to life in prison. Alarmingly her husband, Richard Peete, remained faithful to Louise, writing to her diligently.

While I would like to tell you that he was the one who got away, even jail couldn't protect him from lethal Louise. When she failed to return any of his letters and affection, he committed suicide.

Louise bragged often about her fatal charm. The warden describing her as having "an air of innocent sweetness which masked a heart of ice."

In 1939, almost twenty years after her sentencing Louise received parole with the help of a social worker named Margaret Logan and her husband Arthur. She took on an alias, "Anna Lee" and began working at a servicemen's canteen. Louise lived a quiet life for a few years until she fell back into her old bad habits.

First, her best friend and coworker disappeared. Police found her house ransacked. Louise was called in for questioning since she was a close acquaintance of the deceased. She told police that the lady had sustained severe injuries in an accidental fall and had died. In a baffling turn of events, police took the story at face value and never investigated Louise or even bothered to obtain a death certificate from a coroner.

After Louise's first parole custody overseer died, she was transferred into the care of Margaret and Arthur Logan. Margaret soon disappeared, as people are apt to do when involved with Louise. She told elderly Arthur that his wife was hospitalized and was unable to receive visitors. She then had Arthur committed to an asylum where he died six months after his arrival.

In her signature apathy, Louise donated his body to a medical school for dissection and moved into his house with her new beau, bank manager Lee Judson. If things seemed suspicious to Lee, he never pointed any fingers at Louise. You would think the bullet hole in the wall, the large, fresh mound of dirt in the garden, and a life insurance policy naming Louise as Margaret Logan's sole beneficiary would raise a few red flags. Still, Lee remained silent.

Her new parole officer was not so trusting. The faultless reports of Louise's outstanding behavior, signed in a shaky hand by none other than Margaret Logan were a little too good to be true. Police invaded Louise and Lee's home and discovered a body buried in the garden.

Louise proclaimed that arthritic Arthur Logan had gone insane and beat his wife Margaret to death. Louise, afraid for the old man and herself, bought some time by burying the body in the yard. She then committed Arthur for his own good.

The police didn't buy it. She was charged for the murder and her husband listed as an accessory. Lee was quickly acquitted, but he wouldn't walk the streets a free man for long.

Seemingly still in Louise's lethal grasp, he jumped from the thirteenth floor of an office building the day after his acquittal. Louise chalked it up to him being unable to live without her as she was sentenced to death.

The black widow's reign ended on April 11, 1947, when she was executed by the gas chamber.

XII

Man in the Attic

MURDER FOR LOVE IS A COMMON MOTIVE. BUT no one expects to be murdered by their partner's secret lover who has lived undetected in the attic for years. Walburga, known as Dolly, constructed an elaborate web of lovers and went to great lengths to conceal her relationships.

She even went so far as murder, a staged robbery, and alleged enslavement.

A Bored Housewife and a Secret Boarder

Walburga Korschel was born in Germany and immigrated to the U.S. as a child. She found her Wisconsin farm-life quite dreary and longed to escape the dull days of tending crops and animals. As a teen, Walburga renamed herself "Dolly," and began looking for a way to escape her pastoral surroundings.

Dolly began working at a local apron factory, owned by a fellow German immigrant Fred Oesterreich. Dolly was youthful, outgoing, and charismatic. She quickly charmed the other employees and became fast friends with many of them. It wasn't long until the attractive and jovial Dolly caught the eye of her boss, Fred.

Fred was much older than Dolly, nevertheless the two married when she was only seventeen. At last, Dolly had found her ticket to freedom. Dolly and Fred lived in a lavish house and she could afford nearly every luxury, what more could a woman want? Unfortunately, even though Dolly's surroundings had changed she still found her life dull.

According to her friends, Fred drank a lot and his performance in the bedroom left much to be desired. The latter was point of contention in her marriage and something of great importance to Dolly.

At work, Fred was a demanding, stern, and grumpy boss. Dolly remained a favorite among his workers and could often be found in the office, helping her gruff husband to settle disputes between his employees.

Outside her occasional intermediary duties at the factory, Dolly found her position as a housewife quite drab. She was always on the lookout for more scintillating opportunities, which she found in the form of sexual escapades. She was reported to frequently bring over lovers while her husband was away.

Dolly's most thrilling opportunity showed up on her doorstep one day in the form of seventeen-year-old Otto Sanhuber. He was an employee at her husband's apron factory. Young, impressionable, and insatiable he was just what she had been looking for. Dolly had been complaining to Fred that her sewing machine needed repair and Otto had been sent to fix it. Fred had unknowingly delivered his wife's next sweetheart right into her lap.

Otto began making frequent return visits to the Oesterreich household. Almost daily he was seen coming and going. Dolly couldn't easily explain to her neighbors why she required a handyman so often; instead, she claimed that Otto was her "vagabond half-brother." As you may have guessed, no actual repairs were occurring; Dolly and Otto were engaged in an intense affair.

It became increasingly difficult to hide her relationship both from her neighbors and Fred. Dolly came up with an ingenious solution. The attic of her home was somewhat spacious and livable. It could be accessed through a panel in the closet ceiling of the master bedroom. The same room that she shared with her husband.

Unbelievably, Dolly convinced Otto to quit his job, move into her attic, and enter into a life of hiding.

Dolly set up Otto with a bed, food, a lamp, and even materials to pass the time like books and office supplies. During the day he would see to the needs of the lady of the house, both romantically and otherwise.

At night he read and worked on manuscripts of his own, which Dolly would allegedly mail to publishers for him. Perhaps it was his passion for writing and his dream of becoming a notable science fiction author that made the odd living situation bearable.

Otto never left the attic unless he was given the signal by Dolly. He did not go outside the house, and he never ventured into town. To everyone, except Dolly, it seemed as if he simply disappeared. Fred remained completely oblivious to their new boarder.

Things were going swimmingly for Dolly who had the best of both worlds, a wealthy husband and a young, obedient lover. Then, in 1918, Fred decided the couple was moving to Los Angeles. Dolly agreed to the move on one condition, she would get to choose their new home.

It seemed like a normal request for a housewife, except for the fact that Dolly wanted the one thing most LA homes didn't have, an attic. When she finally found a suitable residence she moved Otto ahead of time, setting him up long before she and Fred ever set foot on the doorstep.

For four years the affair continued. Otto came out in the day and remained in the attic at night, quiet as a ghost. He rarely appeared outside of the home, and certainly didn't leave the attic while Fred was around. Until one day, everything came crashing down.

Attic Man Commits Murder

The couple's marriage had slowly been deteriorating. Fred and Dolly had an all-out brawl on August 22, 1928. The screaming was intense, spurring Dolly's live-in boyfriend into action.

Otto, afraid for Dolly's life, descended from the attic. He ran to the bedroom bureau and retrieved two .25 caliber pistols then made his way to the quarreling couple. One can only imagine what Fred thought when his long-lost employee appeared before him in his home, wielding two guns. They had moved across the country five years ago, how should Otto appear here? Now?

Otto didn't wait for his ex-boss to ask any questions, he shot Fred three times. The older man fell to the floor, dead. Quick-witted Dolly hurriedly staged a robbery scene. She gathered all the cash from the house and Fred's diamond watch and gave it to Otto. She then instructed him to lock her in a closet. Otto headed back up to the attic with the loot and the pistols.

Neighbors who heard the gunshots had called the police. When they burst into the house to find a dead Fred and Dolly locked in the closet, her tale of robbery seemed like the most logical explanation. They did have their suspicions about her involvement but could not explain how Dolly could manage to trap herself in a closet that was locked from the outside.

For eight years after the murder, the affair carried on. Otto remained in the attic, now permitted a typewriter as Fred was no longer around to hear the clacking of the keys. He did not join his lover downstairs and was not allowed to resume a more normal life.

Otto wasn't Dolly's only male friend. She began a romantic relationship with a lawyer she hired after her husband's murder, a Mr. Herman Shapiro.

Shapiro knew nothing of Otto and steadfastly represented Dolly against accusations of murder. Until she presented him with her dead husband's diamond watch that had reportedly been stolen by the murderous robber. Dolly claimed she had found it in the yard.

This was just the start of Dolly's problems. Her love triangle quickly became a web when she took another lover, Roy Klumb. Roy found out about Shapiro. Enraged, he came up with a plan for revenge. He went to the police and told them about how Dolly had given him a pistol not long after the murder and asked him to dispose of it in the La Brea tar pits.

A neighbor, perhaps another scorned lover, came forward to police with a similar story. Dolly had given him a pistol. She told some story about how it too closely resembled the murder weapon and she "did not want to get into trouble," and asked if he could get rid of it. He buried it in his garden.

Police were able to recover both pistols. Even years of decay couldn't prevent ballistics experts from confirming the caliber was a match to the weapons used to kill Fred Oessterich. Dolly was arrested on suspicion of murder.

The Captive Comes Clean

Dolly, in prison and unable to attend to Otto in the attic, confessed her secret to Shapiro. Worried about his wellbeing, she asked Shapiro to deliver him some groceries and check in on him.

When Shapiro and police used the secret code Dolly provided, three taps on the ceiling panel, they were greeted by a thin and pale man. Otto was both friendly and forthcoming, confirming his relationship with Dolly and the part he had played in the death of Fred. Otto was brought in on murder charges.

The press quickly got wind of the story of a murderess who had multiple affairs and even a lover enslaved in her attic. Otto was dubbed the "Attic Man" and "Bat Boy."

In prison, Otto claimed that he was a sex slave, held against his will, and forced to do Dolly's bidding. The jury didn't buy it and found him guilty, only the statute of limitations had long since passed. For the first time in nearly fifteen years, Otto was a free man, no longer having to live a secretive existence. He moved to Canada, changed his name to Walter Klein, and married, fading into obscurity.

Dolly's trial ended in a hung jury. The orchestrator of a web of affairs and even a cover-up for murder, Dolly was released and the charges dropped.

She remained living quietly in LA until her death at the age of eighty.

Conclusion

There you have it, twelve grisly murders of the twenties. we may never know what drove these seemingly normal people to become killers. All we can do is explore their stories and come up with our own individual theories.

We hope you enjoyed reading these spine-chilling accounts and learning about murderers both well-known and long forgotten. We look forward to offering you more hair-raising accounts of history's most ghastly crimes in future volumes.

References

"She Had To Die!" AMERICAN HERITAGE, 1 May 2021, www.americanheritage.com, www.americanheritage.com/she-had-die.

Blanco, Juan Ignacio. "Henry Judd Gray: Murderpedia, the Encyclopedia of Murderers." Henry Judd Gray | Murderpedia, the Encyclopedia of Murderers, murderpedia.org, murderpedia.org/male.G/g/gray-henry-judd.htm.

"Amid Roaring Twenties New Orleans, a Brutal French Quarter Murder." The Historic New Orleans Collection ,25 October 2019, hnoc.org, www.hnoc.org/publications/first-draft/amid-roaring-twenties-new-orleans-brutal-french-quarter-murder-shocked-city.

"JUSTICE STORY: 'Handy man with a knife' flies off the handle." Ny Daily News, 26 April 2020,nydailynews.com,https://www.nydailynews.com/true-crime-justice-story/ny-justice-story-headless-wives-20200426-aexdupfh4fffvcqkxcswdu6tvi-story.html.

"Profile of 'The Jolly Black Widow' Nannie Doss." Thought Co.,17 Oct. 2019, thoughtco.com, www.thoughtco.com/serial-killer-nannie-doss-973101 .

254. "Nannie Doss: Lonely Hearts Serial Killer Puts Us off Internet Dating –.", Film Daily Co., 2 Apr. 2020, filmdaily.co, filmdaily.co/news/nannie-doss.

"The Giggling Granny." ALABAMA HERITAGE, 31 Jan. 2019, alabamaheritage.com, www.alabamaheritage.com/from-the-vault/the-giggling-granny.

"Lady In The Ashes Famous Murder Case in Boston." Celebrate Boston, 27 Oct. 2015, celebrateboston.com, www.celebrateboston.com/crime/lady-in-the-ashes-murder.htm.

Gribben, Mark. "The Butterfly Murders." The Malefactors Register, 27 Jan. 2018, malefactorsregister.com, malefactorsregister.com/wp/the-butterfly-murders.

Deranged, et al. "1920s Archives Premature Burial" Deranged LA Crimes ", 1 Mar. 2021, dreangedlacrimes.com, derangedlacrimes.com/?cat=2.

Baatz, Simon. "Leopold and Loeb's Criminal Minds." Smithsonian Magazine, 1 Aug. 2008, smithsonianmag.com, www.smithsonianmag.com/history/leopold-and-loebs-criminal-minds-996498.

"1924: Leopold and Loeb." Homicide in Chicago 1870–1930, 2012, homicide.northwestern.edu, homicide.northwestern.edu/crimes/leopold.

Bradley, Adam. "Hinterkaifeck Murders: Murder On The Farm." Unsolved Casebook, 27 Jan. 2019, unsolvedcasebook.com, www.unsolvedcasebook.com/hinterkaifeck-murders.

Serena, Katie. "The Gruesome Tale Of The Unsolved Hinterkaifeck Murders." All That's Interesting, 26 Oct. 2018, allthatsinteresting.com, allthatsinteresting.com/hinterkaifeck-murders.

"Here Is the Story of the Wolf Family Murder." Bismarck Tribune, 16 Nov. 1949, bismarcktribune.com, bismarcktribune.com/here-is-the-story-of-the-wolf-family-murder/article_af90320a-4195-5f4a-b145-37fdd83ab5c0.html.

Rasmussen, Cecilia. "Girl's Grisly Killing Had City Residents Up in Arms." Los Angeles Times, 1 Mar. 2019, latimes.com, www.latimes.com/archives/la-xpm-2001-feb-04-me-21037-story.html.

Blanco, Juan Ignacio. "William Edward Hickman | Murderpedia, the Encyclopedia of Murderers." Murderpedia, 2020, murderpedia.org, murderpedia.org/male.H/h/hickman-william.htm.

Renner, Joan. "The Life and Lies of L.A. Man Killer Louise Peete." Los Angeles Magazine, 27 Aug. 2014, lamag.com, www.lamag.com/citythinkblog/the-life-and-lies-of-la-man-killer-louise-peete.

"Louise Peete Archives." Deranged LA Crimes *, 26 Apr. 2017, derangedlacrimes.com, derangedlacrimes.com/?tag=louise-peete.

Nugent, Addison. "The Married Woman Who Kept Her Lover in the Attic." Atlas Obscura, 7 June 2016, atlasobscura.com, www.atlasobscura.com/articles/the-married-woman-who-kept-her-lover-in-the-attic.

Bilyeau, Nancy. "'Attic Man': The 1920s Murder That Shocked Los Angeles." Medium, 16 Sept. 2019, medium.com, tudorscribe.medium.com/attic-man-the-1920s-murder-that-shocked-los-angeles-b9ea73d76c74.

Acknowledgements

This is a special thanks to the following readers who have taken time out of their busy schedule to be part of True Crime Seven Team. Thank you all so much for all the feedbacks and support!

Kim Thurston, Shakila "Kiki" Robinson, Larry J. Field, Linda Blackburn, Michelle Lee, Sue Wallace, Tammy Sittlinger, Tina Rattray-Green, Michele Gosselin, Alicia Gir, Casey Renee Bates, Jennifer Jones, Marcia Heacock, Deirdre Green, Bambi Dawn Goggio, Diane Kourajian, Linda J Evans, Tina Bullard, Jamie Rasmussen, Awilda Roman, Debbie Hill, Nancy Harrison, Wendy Lippard, Matthew Lawson, Bill Willoughby, Alex Slocomb, Bob Carter, Robert Upton, Joey Marie Coulombe, Laura Rouston, Robert Fritsch

Continue Your Exploration Into

The Murderous Minds

Excerpt From True Crime Explicit Volume 1

I
A Troubled Boy

LONG BEFORE HE EVER DRANK THE BLOOD OF people and animals, Richard Trenton Chase lived an unassuming life. Born on May 23rd, 1950, in Santa Clara County, California, to Richard Chase Sr., a computer specialist, and Beatrice, a teacher, Richard appeared in his earliest years to be an average boy—nothing special, though nothing peculiar, either.

When he was three years old, his family managed to afford to move into a house in Sacramento, and the next year, his sister Pamela was born. He was a Cub Scout and played four years of little league baseball. Young Richard was well-liked by his teachers, who all thought he was a sweet child, and he was popular with his peers, with dozens of them coming to attend his birthday parties.

On the surface, the Chases were just like any other family building a life for themselves in mid-century America. However, things at home were a different story.

The 1950s were a polarizing time in American history. Many fondly recall the era's economic prosperity and the growing middle class. It was the age of rock 'n' roll and televisions, but it was also the time when the nuclear family values reigned supreme. Husbands and fathers were the heads of the house, and the rest of the family obeyed. It is little surprise then that, at the time, Richard Chase's childhood was considered to have been unmarred by abuse, especially so when compared to the early lives of other serial killers.

Richard's parents were strict disciplinarians who doled out punishment regularly. When he was only two years old, he was force-fed by his father until he vomited. Pamela Chase would later recall confrontations between her brother and their father that ended with Richard Sr. shaking the boy or throwing him against the wall. The elder Richard was allegedly also emotionally abusive and yelled at his son whenever the boy messed something up.

Due to the elder Richard's difficulty managing money and alcoholism, the parents also had marital problems and often fought, usually loudly, in front of their young children. Beatrice Chase, on the other hand, had the tendency to accuse her husband of "using dope" and trying to poison her. As the years went on, she also began accusing Richard Sr. of infidelity with their neighbors, once even claiming that he was cheating while the family was on a camping trip in Oregon.

Preoccupied with their crumbling marriage, Richard's parents paid little attention to their quiet son and the strange behaviors he began to exhibit. When he was ten years old, Richard developed a grim interest with dead animals. He liked to kill and torture cats that he found around the neighborhood. He was fascinated by their blood and insides in a way that seemed almost clinical.

It started with cats, but Richard would later begin killing birds, rabbits, and dogs. At one point, the young boy had killed so many stray cats that neighbors took notice of their sudden disappearances. Among her flowers, Beatrice found one buried in the soil.

Life got worse at home over the next few years. When he was 12, his parents' fighting reached a boiling point, and his mother saw two different psychiatrists for emotional issues. At 13, his parents went through economic hardship and lost their house. All the while, Richard was still exhibiting troubling behaviors.

When he was around 13, Richard experienced one of his earliest breaks from reality. He became convinced that he was actually a member of the James-Younger Gang, a group of outlaws from the 19th century that included the notorious Jesse James. He got a poster made of the gang that had his picture pasted onto it and repeatedly asked his mother to buy him a cowboy hat.

Richard also developed the strange habit of burning pans while trying to cook for himself in the middle of the night. He tended to leave puddles on the kitchen floor and made messes that he made no effort to clean up. At other times, he would turn the heat up in the house to over 90 degrees whenever he was alone, strip off his clothing, and spend the night lying on the couch in the living room. He liked to play with matches and would often set small fires.

He still wet the bed.

The Macdonald Triad, also known as the Triad of Sociopathy, is a set of behaviors thought to be predictive of violent behavior when observed in childhood. The three behaviors are:

animal cruelty, frequent bed-wetting past the age of five, and arson. Richard exhibited all three.

By the time Richard was in high school, his parents had had enough of each other. They separated, and Beatrice took her children to Los Angeles to live with relatives when Richard was in the middle of ninth grade. Only eight days later, Richard Sr. followed, intent on bringing his son back to Sacramento. Four months later, Beatrice and Pamela came back home.

Back at school, Richard, known as Rick to his classmates, seemed to have no trouble fitting in. He kept himself well-groomed and was decently popular, even going on a few dates with girls.

There were two girls in particular whom he dated seriously, and one relationship he had with a girl named Libby Christopher lasted for an entire year. However, both of these relationships would come to an end for the same embarrassing reason. He was attracted to women, but when it came down to actually having sex, he could not express his attraction. The girls he dated broke up with him once they realized he could not maintain an erection.

Richard was humiliated. Chronically underweight and impotent, he began to feel weak and broken. His defective penis became a point of obsession for him throughout his life and perhaps sparked one of his earliest and most constant delusions.

In Richard's mind, his erectile dysfunction was the cause of a lack of blood. To fix this, he needed to consume the blood of animals.

The End of **The Preview**

Visit us at **truecrimeseven.com** or scan QR Code using your phone's camera app to find more true crime books and other cool goodies.

About True Crime Seven

True Crime Seven is about exploring the stories of the sinful minds in this world. From unknown murderers to well-known serial killers.

Our writers come from all walks of life but with one thing in common and that is they are all true crime enthusiasts. You can learn more about them below:

Ryan Becker is a True Crime author who started his writing journey in late 2016. Like most of you, he loves to explore the process of how individuals turn their darkest fantasies into a reality. Ryan has always had a passion for storytelling. So, writing is the best output for him to combine his fascination with psychology and true crime. It is Ryan's goal for his readers to experience the full immersion with the dark reality of the world just like how he used to do it in his younger days.

Nancy Alyssa Veysey is a writer and author of true crime books, including the bestselling, Mary Flora Bell: The Horrific True Story Behind an Innocent Girl Serial Killer. Her medical degree and work in the field of forensic psychology, along with postgraduate studies in criminal justice, criminology and pre-law, allow her to bring a unique perspective to her writing.

Kurtis-Giles Veysey is a young writer who began his writing career in the fantasy genre. In late 2018, he has parlayed his love and knowledge of history into writing nonfiction accounts of true crime stories which occurred in centuries past. Told from a historical perspective, Kurtis-Giles brings these victims and their killers back to life with vivid descriptions of these heinous crimes.

Kelly Gaines is a writer from Philadelphia. Her passion for storytelling began in childhood and carried into her college career. She received a B.A. in English from Saint Joseph's University in 2016 with a concentration in Writing Studies. Now part of the real world, Kelly enjoys comic books, history documentaries, and a good scary story. In her true crime work, Kelly focuses on the motivations of the killers and backgrounds of the victims to draw a more complete picture of each individual. She deeply enjoys writing for True Crime Seven and looks forward to bringing more spine-tingling tales to readers.

James Parker the pen-name of a young writer from New Jersey who started his writing journey with play-writing. He has always been fascinated with the psychology of murderers and how the media might play a role in their creation. James loves to constantly test out new styles and ideas in his writing so one day he can find something cool and unique to himself.

Brenda Brown is a writer and an illustrator-cartoonist. Her art can be found in books distributed both nationally and internationally. She has also written many books related to her graduate degree in psychology and her minor in history. Like many true crime enthusiasts, she loves exploring the minds of those who see the world as a playground for expressing the darker side of themselves—the side that people usually locked up and hid from scrutiny.

Genoveva Ortiz is a Los Angeles-based writer who began her career writing scary stories while still in college. After receiving a B.A. in English in 2018, she shifted her focus to nonfiction and the real-life horrors of crime and unsolved mysteries. Together with True Crime Seven, she is excited to further explore the world of true crime through a social justice perspective.

You can learn more about us and our writers at:

truecrimeseven.com/about

For updates about new releases, as well as exclusive promotions, join True Crime Seven readers' group and you can also **receive a free book today.** Thank you and see you soon.
Sign up at: **freebook.truecrimeseven.com/**

Or **scan QR Code using your phone's camera app**.

Dark Fantasies Turned Reality

Prepare yourself, we're not going to **hold back on details or cut out any of the gruesome truths...**

Made in the USA
Monee, IL
27 November 2021